For What It's Worth

For What It's Worth

My Liverpool Childhood

BRYAN KELLY

ISIS
LARGE PRINT
Oxford

First published in Great Britain 2006
by
Sutton Publishing Limited

Published in Large Print 2007 by ISIS Publishing Ltd.,
7 Centremead, Osney Mead, Oxford OX2 0ES
by arrangement with
Sutton Publishing Limited

British Library Cataloguing in Publication Data
Kelly, Bryan
 For what it's worth: my Liverpool childhood.
 – Large print ed.
 (Isis reminiscence series)
 1. Kelly, Bryan – Childhood and youth
 2. Large type books
 3. Liverpool (England) – Biography
 4. Liverpool (England) – Social life and
 customs – 20th century
 I. Title
 942.7'53084'092

ISBN 978–0–7531–9412–6 (hb)
ISBN 978–0–7531–9413–3 (pb)

Printed and bound in Great Britain by
T. J. International Ltd., Padstow, Cornwall

To Mama and Dad, I hope that this book conveys my feelings to both of you as you dwell in the mystical regions of outer space.

For the way that you both struggled to raise a worthwhile family during the lean and hungry war years. I think of you both each day as I glide effortlessly through the luxurious abundance of modern life. My love and gratitude goes to both of you — from your eldest son Bryan

Contents

Preface

As an elderly, retired widower free from the constraints of earning a living in order to support myself, my wife and family, my days of heavy industry are a distant memory. My hands have finally healed from the mislaid cloutings of ball-peen-hammers and ill-fitting, open-ended spanners, and the burnt flesh on my body caused by cutting and welding equipment has finally vanished beneath layers of new skin. How now can I fill my time? I have always been an active man and it is imperative that I remain physically fit and mentally alert. I could spend my time in the local pubs swapping yarns with other men my age and although I do like a drink, the heavy smoke-laden atmosphere of crowded watering holes does not appeal to me. I could sit on the canal side and dangle a tasty worm to tempt the hungry fish, but this requires a lot of patience, of which I have very little. I used to enjoy walking my dog on a regular basis, mainly as a form of personal exercise and as a way of meeting people, but my poor four-footed companion has now come to the end of its life. I have also become interested in Latin-American Salsa dancing, its tempo, vigour and vitality appealing to my assertive nature, and so do the ladies. Ever since my first initiation into Salsa I have become a weekly devotee to this vigorous and euphoric form of pleasing and relaxing physical exercise.

I have now decided to record my memories, not

wishing to end up like a forgotten pet dog but to be remembered pleasingly by my many offspring. Writing your memoirs is in itself a wonderful experience; I would certainly recommend it to those who feel they have nothing left in life. The far-distant past comes alive again and you actually seem to relive experiences. Now I am in no way a softie — I am as hard as nails, "a hard knock" they would say in my home town of Liverpool — but delving into the past does something to a man that does not seem quite normal. I find that on occasion it becomes difficult for me to see the screen clearly as the lubricating moisture in my eyes becomes quite excessive, but this in itself, I am sure, is therapeutic; I do not feel sad or lonely but uplifted by these experiences.

A little while ago, one of my daughters introduced me to Mrs Helen Lloyd who is an oral history consultant. While working for the BBC she recorded a condensed version of my life story in a programme called *The Century Speaks*. She has also written a book called *Birmingham Voices* in which a variety of local people, including me, and immigrants were interviewed about their views on migrating to the city. Helen has encouraged me to think that my written memoirs are suitable for publication, and she now acts as my literary agent. She has given me huge personal support and help in producing my book and I will always be indebted to her for this.

This book reveals my life as an infant, then as a kid and on into my teenage years and early adulthood as a soldier. My memories of deprivation, hunger and fear are vivid, as are my recollections of a thirst for knowledge and the people who were strong role models in my life. These people revealed to me the meaning of loyalty, hard work and patriotism. During the Second World War family life, with working-class, loyal and caring parents and many brothers and sisters, was a rich experience. It is thoughts of these folk and our shared lives that has ultimately motivated me to record my early life.

Introduction

My name is John Bryan Kelly. I was born on Sunday 2 September 1931 at Chatham Street Hospital in Liverpool. I was the eldest son and second child of Harold Kelly and Margaret Frances (Peggy) Kelly, née Grant. King George V was our sovereign at the time, and the National Government was in power, under the prime ministership of J. Ramsay MacDonald.

My father was born in St Helen's, just outside Liverpool, and his father, John Kelly, was born in southern Ireland. John Kelly met his future wife, Mary Anne Todd, when he came to St Helen's from impoverished Ireland, like so many others seeking work. Mary Anne Todd was herself of Irish stock although she had been born in St Helen's.

My mother's father, William Grant, was born illegitimately in Wrexham, North Wales. He never knew his father. His grandfather, John Grant, was Scottish and his grandmother was English. Mother's father met his wife, Mary Agnes Chisnall, when he also came to St Helen's looking for work. They were married in St Helen's, then moved on to Liverpool, where they settled down and brought up a family. Mother was the sixth of seven children, the last two being twins.

Mother met Dad, who was the fourth of eleven children, when his family moved to Liverpool. They got married and hoped to settle down, but in their early married life became unanchored itinerants within Liverpool — forever wandering and trying to find a suitable nest in which to set up home and have children. The following is a list of their addresses in Liverpool that I have managed to uncover:

91 Outer Forum
West Derby Road (above the Home and Colonial store)
18 June Road
28 June Road (possibly)
Breck Road (possibly)
Jubilee Drive
20 Fielding Street.

CHAPTER ONE

Memories

As I sit in front of my word processor and marvel at the wonders that science has unveiled for us, I cannot help but be amazed at the computer and its capacity to store information. Yet the human brain's capacity to do likewise far outstrips any computer that has yet been developed. The only problem is the method of retrieval of this information. With the computer, we may know there is information in there somewhere, but we do not know how to access it, having forgotten the program, the key, the file, the code word — how frustrating! The same happens in our minds: we need something to unlock the information, sometimes a sight, a word, a smell, a touch, a sound or a taste will open up a long-forgotten door and retrieve wonderful or terrible memories for us.

I have some mental snapshots of my pre-school days, but they are not necessarily in chronological order; perhaps one day I will be able to arrange them in the correct manner, but for now they are random.

One of my earliest memories was as an infant, lying in my pram — or was it a cot? No, it must have been a pram because I remember that the hood was up. But I have a feeling I was somewhere indoors, and there were a lot of people milling around. It may have been in church at a christening. The one thing that I am certain of was the beautiful and serene face of a woman peering in at me. Somehow I think she was a nun. With all due respect to my mother I know that it was not her. The memory of that beautiful face stayed vividly with me for many a year and well into my adolescence, when it gradually faded away. I still know that it was a beautiful face, but my mind won't recall it in detail anymore.

On another occasion I was a toddler walking with Mother on a wet pavement. I was unhappy, in tears and miserable. Mother tried to hold me by the hand but I rebelled against her. Then I started to fall behind, which made me more miserable. I think it was just the two of us, and the walk seemed interminably long. I imagine the area was Norris Green, a new housing estate on the outskirts of Liverpool. We had just alighted from a tramcar and were making our way to a house in Outer Forum — I now know that Mother and Father lived there at one time with Dad's family. Walking by my mother's side, along the pathway of a large house or office, I was keenly watching a gardener mowing the lawn. The grass must have been quite long because as he moved forward with his machine I could see the edging stones of the pathway appear. The edging stones were in a wave pattern, and I thought that the machine was producing them. The sight of the same type of edging stones today rekindles that early memory.

I recall playing in the street at June Road, which was in Tuebrooke. It must have been springtime because I could smell the blossom of the privet bushes and see their white flowers dropping to the ground.

We lived above a grocery shop, the Home and Colonial stores in West Derby Road, also in Tuebrooke. It was there that I remember sitting on the floor eating cooked cabbage from a dish, and there was something in my mouth that should not have been there: it was a cockroach, which mother removed. She said it must have fallen down the chimney and into the pot as she was cooking over an open fire. Quite understandably, it was many, many years before I would eat cabbage again. Around that time Dad had made a swing out of an old perambulator. He suspended it from the underside of a store that was built over the back yard of the Home and Colonial. Mam and Dad would put me and my sister Monica into the swing and rock us backwards and forwards until we fell asleep.

I also remember riding my small tricycle around at the rear of the Home and Colonial, adjacent to the Salvation Army building. The tricycle had coloured crêpe paper wrapped around the spokes of the wheels, probably to commemorate Empire Day.

I must have been about three when I saw a man up a ladder at the rear of the Home and Colonial. He was pruning a tall tree and he fell off and killed himself, but I don't remember seeing him fall. Someone said that his ladder was resting on the part of the branch that he was sawing off.

From a first-floor window of the Home and Colonial, I remember seeing a military band marching and playing in West Derby Road below. It was probably a parade for the coronation of King George VI in 1936, when I would have been about four years of age. Another memory is being lifted up by Dad to see a large framed photograph that hung above the fireplace. It was of Dad's elder brother, my uncle John Kelly. He was in military uniform and wearing a peaked cap: he served as a private in the 1st Battalion of the Hampshire Regiment, but was killed in the Battle of the Somme.

I also remember watching Dad driving a metal rod into the ground with a hammer in our tiny front garden. I asked him what it was for. He said, "It's an 'earthing rod' for the wireless."

"What do you mean, Dad?" I asked.

He replied, "It's so I can hear the rugby football in Australia."

"Where is Australia, Dad?"

"Right underneath us, son."

That simple statement confused my inadequate young mind for years to come.

I have a distant memory of lying in my cot in June Road. The curtains were drawn but it was light outside. In the street I could hear children playing. I was crying and Mother came upstairs to see what the problem was. It was my elder sister Monica: she was in her cot, next to mine, and having finished drinking her bottle of milk, had climbed into my cot to steal mine. According to Mother it was not the first time she had done this.

There was an alley at the back of our home in June Road, and I recall playing there with a pedal car. The car must have been second-hand because Dad had recently painted it. He did not want me to use it because the paint was still tacky, but I must have made a fuss because for peace and quiet he let me have it. I was very happy pedalling it around the alley until it started to rain and Dad came out to take me and the car inside. I kicked up a fuss again. I can still recall the smell of the wet paint of that little pedal car.

On another occasion I was playing in the back alley in June Road, blowing my whistle, when suddenly the whistle stopped whistling. Aunt Winny, who was looking after me, seemed to panic: she said that I had swallowed the end of it, and took the rest of the whistle from me and threw it over a high wall. This annoyed me. When Mam and Dad came on the scene she recounted the story, as she perceived it. I did not understand what all the fuss was about: I felt quite all right. I told people that I had not swallowed the whistle but Winny insisted that I had. They decided to take me to get checked out, and so a taxi was called and I was whisked away to Alder Hey Children's Hospital. It was nice in the taxi. I don't think I had ever been in one before. By this time it was dark and the street lights were on. I was really enjoying the ride and couldn't understand the concern of my parents. The hospital was nice and so were the nurses. I played on the floor with other children, obviously waiting my turn to see a doctor. I remember being given a chocolate substance to drink and then being put into a bed. I think I was kept in overnight. The following morning I awoke and it was sunny outside — there were large windows, wide open, that led onto balconies. I could see the curtains moving with the morning breeze, revealing well-kept lawns and trees. I was very happy. Then a nurse approached and I was subjected to an enema. I know what an enema is now, but I didn't know then. One end of a tube was inserted into my anus, the other end had a tun dish fitted to it. A nurse filled the tun dish with jugs of warm soapy water, which I could feel flowing inside me. When she had finished I was put into a sitting position and a bed pan was placed underneath me. I could feel my bowels beginning to move and was afraid in case I made a mess of the bed. I told the nurse that the bedpan was full and I needed another, but she reassured me that it was not. I don't know whether they scoured the contents for the missing whistle — this was never revealed to me. Eventually Mam came and took me home; I was reluctant to go because I really liked the hospital, despite the enema.

One night Dad took me to the White City Greyhound Stadium, which was only a short walking distance from our home in June Road. I remember the crowds of men well wrapped up against the cold night air, wearing heavy coats, scarves and caps, and with newspapers stuffed into their pockets. They were smoking cigarettes or tobacco pipes. I particularly liked the smell of pipe tobacco and the exciting atmosphere of the dog track.

Sometimes Dad took me shopping and I was given a penny for my pocket money. Once, I bought a ring of four scones with it from the cake shop. I felt very excited about this transaction as it was the first thing that I had ever bought and I couldn't get home fast enough to give them to my mother. I remember how pleased she was.

On another shopping trip, with Mother, I wandered off on my own. I was found some streets away happily playing in the sunshine in a heap of builders' sand, completely unconcerned about being alone and unsupervised.

I went to Newsham Park once without permission. To get there involved crossing a busy road. I asked Dad if I could go and he had said no, not on my own; but I went anyway. I was enjoying myself walking and running about, oblivious to any danger. There was the smell of burning twigs and leaves as I watched the gardeners tidying up, so it must have been autumn. Eventually a search party of aunts and my parents found me.

Another recollection is of Aunt Winny taking me for a stroll through Newsham Park — I think she used me for an excuse to get out herself. On the way back she stopped to talk to a man, and they stood outside some lock-up garages. I seemed to be standing around for ages before we moved off home again. I wondered what people talked about — it seemed a waste of time to my young mind, when there were more important things to do like running about and jumping up and down.

At our house in June Road I fell down the stairs. Mother said that I told her Grandma Kelly had pushed me. I cannot remember but I do know that Grandma was standing behind me polishing the balustrade and I probably wasn't quick enough to move out of her way. Grandma Kelly was known as a bit of a tyrant and would splash holy water all over the house if things didn't seem to be in order. She had religious icons hanging on the walls, standing on shelves and fastened to the backs of doors. I can never remember seeing her smile or being pleasant to me — she doesn't stand out in my memory as you would expect your grandmother to. Perhaps it was the culmination of living a very hard life and bringing up eleven children, coupled with the fact that she was a widow. She also had to endure the loss of her eldest son in the First World War, and the stigma of having another son in a mental institution.

I remember going for walks with Dad. On our way home on one occasion it was dark, the pavements were wet and the street gaslights were lit. The shop windows were illuminated and the streets were busy with people hastening along their way. There were horses and carts with oil lanterns hanging from the backs and other men pushing hand carts. I remember gazing at a very large wooden structure, an advertisement hoarding. I was marvelling at the huge timbers used to make the framework that supported the hoarding. Another time we were strolling on some common land near a brook. I saw a gypsy woman and an old horse-drawn caravan which was parked for the night. Their horse was grazing on the grassland and on an embankment a steam train was passing by. Some children were playing in the brook, but I was not allowed to join them.

As a todder I remember going along to church with Dad in Green Lane and watching the priest swinging the incense container on its long chain. The smell wafted towards me and I found it was a very pleasant and memorable aroma.

CHAPTER
TWO

Infant School & June Road

I was being taken by the hand by my mother to my first school, St Cecilia's in Tuebrook. As we made our way across the playground a contraption standing out on its own caught my eye.

"What's that, Mam?", I asked.

"It's the school board," she replied. This was in effect a blackboard resting on an easel, probably for outside lessons, because it was summertime. I enjoyed school especially at Christmas time and when the lights were on, but like all children at times of peakiness, sometimes I didn't want to go to school. When this happened Mother would threaten me by saying "the School Board" will come for you, meaning of course a person from the school authorities. I immediately saw the vision of the contraption I saw in the playground on the first day that I went to school. I was in a dilemma: my child's mind could not comprehend how an inanimate object could come along and collect me even though it had three legs. I never questioned my mother on this topic but pondered over it for years until such time that my mind had developed enough to solve the enigma.

There were many herbalists' shops in Liverpool in those days and Dad had always taken a keen interest in herbal medicine. It was probably a lot cheaper for the working class to visit the herbalist's than to consult the doctor. If any of the family had bad colds or a severe cough he would have the remedy, making us an infusion of elderflowers and peppermint, or raspberry tea, or even ginger root boiled in beer.

"Get this down you and then go straight to bed," he would command, "and it will sweat the illness out of you." Other pet phrases he had when we were feeling low in health were: "Are your bowels open? Have you been today? Has he been, Peggy?"

"How would I know? I don't follow him to the lavatory, he's a big lad now," Mother would say.

Dad's remedy for this particular malady was either Castaretts, a well-known laxative, or syrup of figs. I don't know which one he gave me on this occasion, but I think he might have dosed me with both, to be on the safe side: I suppose he was what you might term a belt and braces man. The next day at infant school as I sat quietly at my desk listening to the teacher, my bowels started to open. I just could not control the movement. I was hoping nobody would notice my predicament, especially the little girl sitting next to me. It was a warm and soft sensation and a relief as it slowly left my body. I was soon sitting on a soft, and comfortable, cushion of excrement, and the cushion was increasing in size as I sat there. The putrid smell had reached my nostrils and so it must also have reached the little girl sitting next to me and spread its noxious odour to the rest of the confined class of children, including the teacher. Although I was young I was aware of my plight and just sat motionless (but not motion-less), watching the teacher, but without any response. Mid-morning came and the school bell rang out: it was time for us children to have a break from lessons and relax in the open air of the playground. Everybody stood up from their desks and hurriedly left the room, except me of course. The teacher sensed that something was amiss and walked over to me.

"Aren't you going outside to play, Bryan?" she asked.

"Errr, no, Miss," I meekly responded.

"Is there something wrong?" she enquired. It was quite obvious that something was wrong — as she stood over me the smell was all-pervading.

"I think I had better get your big sister to walk you home," she suggested.

It was fortunate that Monica went to the same school, or I don't know what would have happened. Mother could not have been contacted as ordinary people did not have telephones and very few had cars. The teacher left the classroom, and then returned with Monica.

"Will you be able to take your brother home?" she enquired of Monica.

"Yes, Miss." I must have been five or six years of age and my sister about six or seven. I awkwardly raised myself from the wooden bench at the command of teacher and stood next to my sister in the aisle. I wore short trousers and the excrement was running down the back of my legs and into my stockings; it was also on the seat of my desk and on the polished floor. Monica took me by the hand and led me gingerly out of the classroom, out of the school and onto the street. Holding me gently by the hand she walked beside me along an avenue of middle-class houses. It was summer, the sun was shining and it was very hot. I then became an immediate target for marauding flies who homed in on me from all sides — I was a free and open banquet to them. People passed us by with peculiar looks on their frowning faces, some pitying, others shocked. My sister was terribly concerned for me but I just calmly accepted the situation: embarrassment was not yet known to me. For all her young years my sister was undaunted although we had more than a mile to walk before we would reach home. Her inborn mothering instinct, which was to materialise many years later when she brought up a fine family of her own, showed its seed that day.

"Bryan, I'll walk in front of you," she said, "and you walk behind me but walk backwards so that nobody can see your legs."

Now that was a very good idea in principle but not very easy to implement, for I was swaying all over the pavement because I could not see where I was walking. Then Monica modified her idea.

"You walk forwards in front of me, Bryan, and I'll walk right behind you."

"But I don't know the way, Micky," I protested.

15

"Don't you worry about that, Bryan, I'll show you the way," she replied.

So we both progressed painfully slowly along the middle-class avenue and onto the main West Derby Road with all its open shops and crowds of shoppers. Hundreds of people must have witnessed the spectacle that we presented, but no one asked any questions or interfered in any way — they just gave us those peculiar looks and kept their distance. I remember a big friendly dog running up and sniffing me and I bent down to stroke its back. "Don't do that, Bryan, or he'll follow us home," scolded Micky.

We finally reached home and made our entrance from the rear, which was customary. It was a relief for me and especially my sister. But what a surprise for Mother, Grandmother and aunts! They were all in the back yard doing the weekly washing, and the place was a hive of activity. They were shocked to find us home without being collected, and doubly shocked to find the reason. I was told to stand still and not to move until the washing was completed. This was understandable as I must have left an obvious trail for the last mile or so of my journey.

Dirty washing was being boiled in a boiler, which was a cast-iron bowl about 2 or 3ft in diameter. The bowl had a rim that rested on brickwork about 3ft off the ground and beneath the bowl was a fireplace. This was the means by which the water was boiled. Coal or coke would be put on the fire along with old boots and shoes and indeed anything that would burn. This was long before the clean air act of today came into being.

When the washing had been boiled it was transferred to a Dolly tub. This was a zinc-coated steel barrel into which a Dolly would be placed, a three-legged stool with a long vertical prop rising from its centre. A cross-member was attached to the vertical prop about 6in from its end, and the whole would be about 4ft tall. By grasping the cross-member with both hands you would turn the Dolly clockwise then anti-clockwise continuously: this action would agitate the dirty washing in the tub. When sufficient agitation had been administered, which was probably measured by the aching arms of the operative, the clothes were transferred to a zinc bath full of cold water: this was the rinsing process, and from here the sopping clothes went into the mangle, a very heavy cast-iron monstrosity with two horizontal wooden rollers. You could adjust the distance between the rollers by turning a wheel on top of the mangle, and the closer the rollers were the more water you could squeeze out of the soaking-wet washing, but an optimum distance was achieved by folding the thinner clothes and opening out the thicker clothes, which also prevented the crushing of buttons, buckles and the like. The rollers were turned by a cranking handle on the right-hand side of the mangle. Sometimes two women would operate the mangle, one turning the handle and the other feeding the rollers with washing. When the washing had passed through the machine it was put on a table before being pegged out on the line.

On laundry days the yard would be awash with water and the air full of steam. It was vital that a nice clear day was selected and preferably a sunny one too — Mother Nature was needed to dry the clothes, otherwise they had to be taken indoors and put around fire guards and a contraption suspended from the ceiling, which was in effect a tall clothes horse. The contraption could be lowered for loading it with damp washing, then it would be pulled aloft by a pulley system in order to dry in the ambient heat of the kitchen. I suppose this was a vast improvement on the method that still exists in some areas of the world of bashing your washing on rocks near a river, but it was hardship compared to the Western world today, where even the poorest of us live in luxury. I admired the ordinary women of yesteryear, who were strong and tough and worked hard yet still retained their femininity.

Meanwhile, I stood around quietly and obediently in my personal filth, watching and studying the industrious women and making sure that I never got in their way. Then my turn came to be cleansed. "Oh! Deary deary me!" exclaimed my mother as my filthy clothes were stripped off and placed into the boiler. I was then placed unceremoniously into the Dolly tub with its warm but dirty water, to sounds of hysterical laughter coming from the women. As I was thoroughly washed down it was pleasant to be unburdened from the malady that had been with me for the last two hours or more, and I was thankful that the Dolly had not been used on me. Father was upstairs in bed trying to get some rest despite the noise from all this domestic industry, and especially the rattling mangle — the rest was his respite from being on night shift at the

Liverpool docks. After being taken from the Dolly tub I was dried, wrapped in a blanket and carried upstairs and placed beside my father. Mother told him what had happened and said, "If Bryan happens to shit on you, then you have only yourself to blame." But I am sure I did not. I was now fully unloaded like a cargo ship high and dry, with my Plimsoll line well out of the water and even my bilges pumped dry. Dad cuddled me closely: I was happy, warm and contented and I immediately fell sound asleep.

CHAPTER
THREE

Fielding Street

The family left Grandma's house, 18 June Road, in the summer of 1938. We then moved to 20 Fielding Street, Liverpool 6. Dad hired a rather small removal van to transport our possessions, and all our furniture and belongings, which did not amount to very much, were loaded into it. Dad, my sister Monica and brother Gerald managed to squeeze in as well. There was no room left for the rest of us so Mother, myself and brother Peter in his pram, together with a bowl of goldfish, had to walk. It was quite a journey for me. We travelled through Newsham Park, which was nice because it was sunny, then along Boaler Street, Farnworth Street, down Romilly Street, then turned left into Fielding Street — a journey of about 2 miles. When we eventually arrived the removal van had been and gone and our meagre possessions had been unloaded and carried into our new home.

Fielding Street was probably named after the novelist, Henry Fielding. It was a rather drab street (but far from the worst in Liverpool), consisting of working-class terraced houses two storeys high, each with a bay window and without a garden. At the south

end of the street and on the corner of Kensington was
the Royal Arch public house and opposite was a
grocer's, Scott's, above which was the Kensington
Gym. At the northern end was a little sweet shop run
by two old ladies — we kids referred to it as Miss
Mack's Muck Shop — and next to that was Ernie
Bradbury's yard and his mother's house and shop. Our
house, No. 20, had three bedrooms with a coal fireplace
in every room; there was no central heating in those
days, no bathroom, no indoor toilet and no hot water,
but as Dad would say, "we had hot and cold running
bugs". In the back kitchen there was a basic brass cold
water tap with lead piping. This was fixed to the untiled
wall above a brown rectangular earthenware sink,
which was supported on brick piers. There was also a
cast-iron washing boiler. In the kitchen or living room
there was a cast-iron fireplace with an oven to the right,
and within the oven was a quite heavy but removable
iron shelf, which we called "the plate". In the cold
winters to come this shelf would be the object of much
discussion, deliberation and argument. It was a prized
possession that we kids verbally fought over. We would
wrap it carefully in an old piece of blanket and take it
with us upstairs to our freezing bedroom. Placed
carefully within the covers of the uninviting bed and at
our feet it was the ultimate in luxury and transformed
the bed into a warm and cosy nest. I always remember
that Monica was the first one to try it out.

"You have it tonight, Micky, and bring it down in the
morning so that Bryan can use it tomorrow night,"
Mam would say. The iron shelf would be completely

forgotten during the course of the next day until the bitter chill of the evening drew closer. We would huddle around the open fire wearing our jackets or even overcoats, and would jockey for the best positions around the fire, sitting as close as possible to absorb the maximum heat. I always wondered why our backs were so cold, and now realise it was because the fire drew in cold air from outside through gaps and cracks in the doors and floors, then would hit our backs, feed the fire with oxygen and race up the chimney in a continuous cycle of cold and icy draughts. But it had its compensations, since houses in those days never suffered with mildew.

"Come on, move away from it!" Mother would command, "And let your father put more coal on."

"Come on now, you lot, it's time for bed," Mother would say.

"My turn for the plate!" I would remind everybody, anticipating a luxurious warm and cosy bed.

"Take it out of the oven then, Bryan, and watch you don't burn yourself," Mam would say.

I opened the black iron door of the oven, at the same time asking "Where is the blanket, Micky?" The oven was empty: "There's no shelf, Mam!" I screamed.

"Monica, didn't you bring the shelf down this morning?" Mother asked.

"No, sorry, Mam, I forgot." It took all day for the shelf to absorb the heat from the oven so I had to forgo my night of anticipated luxury and suffer the discomfort of the icy sheets. As time progressed we would remind each other to bring the shelf down and replace it in the oven. The system usually worked but Monica was mostly to blame for any lapse of organisation.

Above the oven was a ledge and set into the wall was a damper — if you pulled the damper out it diverted hot combustion gases from the fire to the back of the oven, thereby giving it extra heat. To the left of the fire was a hob, which also had a damper. There was always a full iron kettle resting on the hob. It had a round earthenware ball inside about 1 inch wide to prevent lime-scale deposits building up. Above the fireplace was a mantelpiece with a mantleshelf, and under the mantleshelf was a brass rail for hanging clothes to dry. There was a brass retainer in front of the ash pit, and a brass fender surrounding the fireplace. Built into the ends of the fender were brass boxes with upholstered leather hinged tops, which contained wood chips and waste paper (or fire lighters if you were posh) for starting the fire — and of course we would sit on the upholstered box tops, unless the fireguard was around the fire, as it often was. When the fire was lit and glowing red and the black ironwork was polished (with Zebo) and the brass work polished (with Brasso), the whole scene was a beautiful picture in itself. But it was hard work keeping it that way. Each room of the house had a gaslight suspended from the ceiling, but to light it you had to fit a delicate mantle to the gas outlet pipe, pull a chain connected to a lever enabling gas to flow to the mantle, then apply a lighted taper — finally it would ignite and give off a brilliant white light.

At the rear of the house was a paved yard, and at the bottom of the yard was the lavatory, which had a rickety door with large gaps at the top and bottom. These were both for ventilation and to let daylight in. A large 6in nail knocked into the brick wall was regularly replenished with squares of old newspaper that often smelled of fish and chips. Outside the toilet and built into the external wall was the bin for fire ash and general rubbish. There was not a lot of rubbish in those days because whatever could be burned was put on the fire — old footwear, for instance, and potato peelings. Nor was there as much tinned food about as there is today, and pre-packed food was minimal. Lemonade bottles, milk bottles and jamjars were refundable, so what was thrown away was absolute rubbish.

Since we did not live in a throw-away society, we children mostly dressed in hand-me-downs — the expression in Liverpool was "First up, best dressed". Dad would always cut the boys' hair and he would also repair our boots. He had a cobbler's last and all the necessary tools. Mother was very good at sewing, embroidery, knitting and dressmaking. With these skills she was constantly on the go repairing our clothes and making new ones. Because television had not yet become commonplace in the home, the wireless set was our means of keeping in touch with the outside world. In their spare time Dad and Mam would listen to the wireless, but although they were sitting down they would be doing something useful, Dad cobbling our boots or cutting our hair, Mam knitting or darning our socks, or combing our hair with a Derback comb looking for nits and lice — and she would find plenty. Head lice were very common among young children and the nit nurse would regularly visit schools and check the kids' heads. When she found something that should not be there she would give a note to the child to take home. My sister Monica and I regularly brought notes home and Mother had a full-time job trying to keep our heads free of the vermin. Mother would put an old newspaper on the floor and comb our heads over it with the Derback comb; lice would fall onto the paper and Mother would kill them between her thumb nails.

The wireless was powered by an accumulator and a large, dry battery. The accumulator was, in effect, a battery, so why the wireless needed two batteries I could not figure out. What I do know is that the accumulator, which was about 8in high with a 6in base, was made of thick glass and had a metallic carrying handle fitted to it. It had to be recharged very frequently. This was done at the chandler's store in Kensington. One day I was sent on an errand to collect the recharged accumulator, but I had a mishap on the way home: through my ungainliness and clumsiness it dropped from my hand and fell to the pavement, whereupon it smashed into small pieces. The acid contents then splattered over my boots and stockings. When I returned home carrying just the handle, with a shocked look on his face, Dad scolded me for being such a fool and Mother scolded me even more for burning my clothes.

Dad used to tinker with the wireless and told me that years earlier when the wireless first came out he had made a crystal wireless set, which was known as a cat's whisker — and you needed head phones to listen into it. He erected a 30ft metal tube at the bottom of our yard securely fastened to the back wall: this was his aerial post, and from the top he had a wire aerial leading into the back of his wireless set. The wire was supported from the house top with other cables and glazed insulators.

Dad had been interested in rugby since he was a lad in St Helen's, and this was the team he supported. But he also supported Liverpool Stanley, and of course Liverpool Football Club, and on occasions he took me to see all three. He would be tinkering with the control knobs of his beloved wireless endeavouring to pick up rugby broadcasts from the other side of the world.

"Ooooooh . . . Ooooooh" — a peculiar sound would be heard coming from the wireless followed by the distant sound of a football commentator's voice speaking in English but with an accent I had not heard before, then "Ooooooh . . . Ooooooh", then back again to the commentator and the roar of a huge crowd. Dad would be excited with all this and happy that he had picked up the match; I stood watching him and tried to understand his jubilant excitement.

"Do you know where this is coming from, son?" he would question.

"No, Dad," I replied.

"Australia, son — Australia — all the way from sunny Australia."

26

"Ooooooh . . . Oooooooh."

"What's that funny noise, Dad?" I enquired.

"That is oscillating, son, oscillating — friggin' nuisance it is — friggin' nuisance. I'll have to get a longer aerial, son. A longer aerial."

CHAPTER
FOUR

Diphtheria

It was high summer and yet I was cold and shivery, practically sitting on top of the kitchen fire and leaning over the fire guard. Dad had just arrived home from work. "What's wrong with that lad, why isn't he outside playing in the street?" he said to Mother.

"I don't know, he's been like that all day," she responded.

"What's wrong, lad, why aren't you outside playing in the sunshine?" Dad said to me.

"I feel sick, Dad." I answered.

Dad said we had better get the doctor in to have a look at me. He asked Mrs Jones across the other side of our street if he could use her telephone, and Mrs Jones obliged. She was one of only two persons in the street to have a telephone. Her husband was a small building contractor who had a lockup garage with a yard at the end of the street, and he was also mobile: he had a hand cart in which he used to carry his tools and material about. The other person with a telephone (they weren't called phones in those days) was Mrs Bradbury, mother of Ernie Bradbury, who lived at the other end of the street which butted onto Romilly

Street at right angles. The little shop that she ran sold dairy products and was part of a big yard with stables for ponies and stables for cows — they called the part that had the cows the "shippin". I cannot find any dictionary reference to shippin associated with cows, so I wonder if at one time sheep were kept there and it was a sheep pen, the name becoming distorted over the intervening years. Anyway, the doctor called and he took swabs of mucus from the back of my throat and from my nose, and sent them away to be analysed. I think it was the following day that the results were confirmed, but it might have been longer. The upshot was, it was clear I had contracted the deadly diphtheria germ, and so I was kept in bed until the ambulance arrived to take me to hospital. When the neighbours found out that I had contracted the disease they told Mother that I had been poking a long pole down the openings in a sewer cover in the middle of the street, which indeed I had — just one of the silly pranks that kids get up to, without any knowledge of the filth that exists there, or the fact that rats who carry disease live down there. The act of retrieving the slimy pole with my bare hands and eating food afterwards without washing was probably the cause of the disease. When I was waiting for the ambulance I heard the noise of a heavy lorry in the street and jumped from my bed to see what it was, as vehicles were a curiosity in the street. It was a suction machine for cleaning out the drains. I remember thinking how efficient the corporation was, or was it just a coincidence that it was in our street at that time?

In any case, I was taken to Netherfield Road Isolation Hospital in the Everton district of Liverpool. For some reason known only to medical science, the foot end of my bed was raised on wooden blocks which were put under the legs, so that my head was lower than my legs. That night I seemed to be in a delirium, possibly as a result of medication, with things floating around my head. Next day I was fed with liquid through an earthenware pot with a spout. I don't remember having any visitors other than Dad, and even he was not allowed to enter the ward: the nurse pointed him out to me as he stood the other side of a closed glass door. He had probably called in on his way home from work, and we waved to each other momentarily before he set off again. The side of the ward that I was on was for children suffering from diphtheria, and the other side for children suffering from scarlet fever, another deadly disease.

I was in hospital for nine weeks, and even had my eighth birthday there. I got some sort of present — a cuddly toy I think — but I was not allowed to play with it; instead, it was put on a table in the middle of the ward where I could look at it. The day after my birthday Britain declared war on Germany. The first I knew of the war was when the daylight from the windows opposite my bed was gradually diminished. Men outside were building up walls of sandbags to minimise possible lacerations to patients caused by flying glass from exploding bombs. After about eight weeks I was helped from my bed onto my feet by two nurses. I could not walk, having been confined to bed for so long a period. I was escorted up and down the ward so that my legs could regain strength, and after a few days I was escorted outside the ward onto an area of tarmac with railings around it. The hospital was built on high ground — I think it was known as St George's Heights — and had a panoramic view of the River Mersey and dockland. It was very nice and refreshing to be outside in the chill air after being incarcerated for so long in a stuffy hospital ward. It was November and the river area was misty. I could hear the sound of ships' fog horns as they made their way cautiously up and down the busy river.

When the doctor deemed that I was fit enough to leave the hospital Mother was informed somehow, since on her next visit she brought my clothes. I was well muffled up, then left the hospital and we headed home by tramcar.

Everybody remarked on how thin I was, especially my legs which were like matchsticks. Dad said he thought I had rickets. I remember that dark evening sitting around the table with the family waiting for our evening meal. The wireless was on as usual and the news was all about the war. Dad came in from work holding the *Liverpool Echo*, the evening newspaper.

"We are going to be rationed, Peggy," he said to Mother.

"Oh, is that good?" I asked.

"No, it bloody well isn't!" Mother replied.

"There's no need for that language in front of the children," said Dad. He did not like foul language of any sort. I don't remember him ever swearing coarsely, and certainly not in front of us — frig this and frig that was his only expression of distaste. Rationing was then explained to us as we sat around the table.

"You won't be able to waste any food at all," Mother said, "because we will not be getting a lot so whatever you get on your plate you will eat. We might not know where our next meal is coming from." Mother was obviously concerned, hence her strong language. She had a family to feed and the primitive instincts of a mother under duress were brought to the fore.

Dad said, "I'll get an allotment and grow my own vegetables."

"What's an allotment, Dad?" I asked.

"It's a piece of ground that you rent off the corporation," Dad explained.

"Oh, that sounds good! . . . Can I come with you and help?"

"Certainly you can, son. It'll be hard work but the exercise will build you up and you'll be out in the fresh air away from these dirty streets."

CHAPTER
FIVE

Junior School

With my sister Monica I attended the Roman Catholic
Canon Kennedy Memorial School in Edge Lane. The
teachers were nuns and wore the traditional black habit
from neck to ankle and a white starched front piece
with a shawl draped across their shoulders. They also
carried a broad belt around their waists from which
hung a set of rosary beads and a crucifix. On their
heads they wore a black headdress with a white
starched cap beneath, so that no hair was to be seen.
The headmistress was a big lady called Sister Mary
Ignatius, whom Dad in his humorous moments would
refer to as Sister Mary Good Gracious.

"Is Sister Mary Good Gracious still there, Bryan?"
he would ask.

"It's not Good Gracious, Dad, it's Hignatus," I
would knowingly explain.

"Oh! I see, so she's changed her name has she?" he
would question.

"Take no notice of your dad, Bryan, he's pulling your
leg," Mam would say.

I don't remember much about this school apart from
the fact that I always seemed to be saying prayers and

listening to religious instruction. After I had recovered from diphtheria and left the hospital I returned to Canon Kennedy School, but something peculiar seemed to have happened: I was ostracised by the teachers. Did they think that I still carried the disease? Whatever the reason, I was isolated for a week or two without lessons, and instead was put to work in the vegetable garden at the back of the school. Here I was given a wheelbarrow and a rake and told to rake the ground, which was very hard as it was November, and collect up the stones, then put them into the wheelbarrow. When the wheelbarrow was full I had to push it through a gate that was set in the back wall of the school and tip it among the bushes in the local park. I was in effect tipping the stones at the rear of Kensington Gardens. Perhaps the teachers, on seeing how rundown my body was, were trying to help me regain my strength, but it was a peculiar existence being there in the garden all on my own at such a young age. I was already hopelessly behind in lessons compared to the other children so that when I did recommence classroom learning I was completely lost. And this had a profound effect on my self-esteem, giving me a feeling of inadequacy and a lack of self-confidence that stayed with me well into my teenage years.

CHAPTER
SIX

The Phoney War

In the period known as the Phoney War, German mines and U-boats sank British shipping, mainly in the North Atlantic Ocean. These ships brought vital raw materials and food supplies to our shores. The German plan was to blockade the country and starve us into submission. At this time Britain was a world power with a huge empire and dominions spread throughout the globe. Both her Royal Navy and her Merchant Navy were the largest in the world, and at any one time there were 2,500 British merchant ships sailing the seven seas.

The German armies rapidly advanced over eastern and western Europe. The British Expeditionary Force that had gone to France was pushed back to the coast, together with the remnants of the French army it had gone to assist. I took a keen interest in the war and listened intently to the wireless, and although I could not read I could gather what was happening by looking at the maps that were printed in the newspapers. I was mesmerised by the broad black arrows showing the German advances and the smaller white arrows showing the Allied retreats.

Mother was issued with her ration books. They were brown in colour and she had one for each of us, but babies had a green one. She had to register with one grocer only and that was where she would get her weekly supply of food that was rationed by weight: butter, margarine, cheese, bacon, tea, lard and sugar. Eggs were rationed according to their availability, with priority given to babies who had a green ration book. Meat was rationed by price because some meat products were more expensive than others. Clothes were rationed with coupons. Petrol was only issued to those with special needs, like doctors and solicitors — the toffs. A Ministry of Propaganda and a Ministry of Food were created. People were urged to eat more potatoes as these were readily available and did not have to be imported. Adverts showed a character shaped like a potato called Potato Pete. We were also urged to eat plenty of carrots and were told that they were good for our eyesight — encouraged by the fact that night fighter pilots ate plenty of them to help them see in the dark. There were all kinds of tips on how to make food go further, how to sweeten without sugar, how to make chocolate cake without chocolate and so on. Any leftovers such as peelings and stalks were put into swill bins in the street, and the contents taken away to feed some farmers' pigs.

Dad was a very hard worker. He had been given his allotment in a place called Knotty Ash, which was situated on the eastern outskirts of Liverpool. He built himself a small tool shed from odd scraps of timber and rigged it up with a paraffin heater that he used for boiling water to make a pot of tea. I loved going up there with him on the No. 10 tramcar to work the land together. Any time at all that Dad had to spare we would be grafting on the allotment. He grew a wide variety of vegetables and even fruits such as strawberries, raspberries and of course rhubarb. Mother was a good cook, and on occasions she would bake her own bread. I would watch the dough with fascination as it expanded while resting in front of the open fire in a large bowl covered with a damp cloth. When it was ready Mam would knead it and shape it into loaves, then bake the bread in the oven next to the fire. What a wonderful smell exuded from that oven and what a delight to eat! And it was so much nicer than the wartime loaf of black bread. She would also make apple pie. Monica and I would squabble over who had the right to lick clean the mixing bowl used for the dough, and we would also squabble over the cooking apple peelings. We must have been hungry because nothing was wasted. I would eat raw rhubarb and cabbage, while my brother Gerald's delicacy was the uncooked rind from the bacon ration. We had a joint of meat once a week, usually a leg of lamb for Sunday dinner. Mother would roast it, then carve all the meat from the bone. At that time we had a scrawny dog named Spot who sat there patiently watching and waiting in anticipation of its delicacy, as dogs are wont to do. When Mother was satisfied that the bone was bare she would throw it to Spot — but he never stood a chance, as I was there like a shot: I was first in the order of nibbling.

"Oh Bryan, let the dog have his bone!" Mother would exclaim.

"I will, Mam, there's too much meat on it yet for the dog. I'll give it to him in a minute." When I had picked clean every last morsel of flesh from the bone then I reluctantly gave it to the drooling and obedient dog who sat on his haunches watching my every movement. It was tough being a dog in those days. Dogs were not issued with ration books and were looked upon as a standby source of protein themselves — as was the case in the siege of Warsaw, where they ate anything, even rats, and where some even resorted to cannibalism. The only problem with eating your pet dog was the sheer waste: who would you give the bones to?

Throughout the duration of the war we never saw tropical fruit such as oranges, bananas, pineapples, lemons or grapefruit. But we did get concentrated orange juice in cartons, together with tins of dried milk and packets of egg powder, mostly imported from the USA, provided the ships got through the blockade. Dried and salted fish was quite common and so was horse and whale meat.

The blackout was one of the first austerity measures imposed on the populace in this period. No interior light was allowed to penetrate outside after lighting-up time, which was published daily in the press — even smoking outside or lighting up was taboo. Another austerity measure was the silencing of church bells, which would only peal again if Britain was invaded by land forces or paratroopers, or in the event of victory. A further sign of war was the removal of all road signs and markings in order to make it more difficult for enemy agents to know where they were if they were to land by parachute.

CHAPTER
SEVEN

The Blitz

Before the mass bombings of Liverpool and Merseyside there were fifty-seven smaller air raids. The following extracts from official sources show details of some of these raids:

1940 5 June, first air-raid siren alert. No bombs dropped
28-9 July
1 August
9 August, first casualty
10 August
17-18 August
28 August
29 August
30 August
31 August
20 September, light air raids
15 October, light air raids
8 November, light air raids
28 November, 150 bombers, Durning Rd; Sch; bombed with many casualties; Mam's brother, Thomas Joseph Grant, was in attendance as air-raid warden

20 December, 500 bombers over three nights,
    6.30p.m. to 4 a.m.
21 December
23 December

1941 3 January
15 February
24 February
12 March, 9p.m. to 3 a.m.
13-21 March, 250 bombers over two nights
14 March
7 April
15 April
26 April
1 May, Thursday, 800 bombers over eight nights
    11p.m. to 1 a.m.
2 May, 50 bombers
3 May
4 May
5 May
6 May
7 May
8 May

1942 10 January, last air raid on Merseyside

In total, there were over 200 air raids on Liverpool and Merseyside during the war, with 4,100 civilians killed and 76,000 people made homeless. Before air-raid shelters were built people had to fend for themselves as best they could. Dad went to work as usual on the docks, busily unloading the cargoes, while I would help Mother to prepare for the evening air raid.

Of course we never knew if there would be a raid or not. People developed the habit of looking at the night sky and trying to determine the possibility of an air raid.

"They won't be over tonight," Dad would say, looking up at the sky.

"How do you know, Dad?" I would ask.

"There's too much cloud about. They won't be able to find their way here or hit their targets." I was always confused by these statements because on other occasions Dad would say something completely different.

"There'll be no bombers over tonight, son."

"How can you tell, Dad?"

"Well, look for yourself. It's a clear sky, which means the searchlight crews and the ack-ack gunners can spot them. No, they won't be over tonight — they wouldn't dare."

The next minute the sirens would be howling and all hell would be let loose.

"I thought you said there would be no raid tonight?" said Mother quizzically.

"Ha! Well, they weren't listening to me," Dad would retort.

"I should think not!" said Mother. "They're listening to Hermann Göring instead." Dad was always slipping on banana skins and ending up with egg on his face, and Mam was always quick to humorously rub it in.

Sometimes the sound of the air-raid sirens would be followed by a period of anxious waiting while nothing happened; then the all-clear would blast out. It was decided that the kitchen, being sandwiched between the parlour and the back kitchen, was the safest place to shelter, and so here we made a tent-like structure, where the family slept night after night during the May blitz. This meant that the kitchen in effect became the living room, and that most of the cooking took place in the back kitchen.

Our method of protection, if you can call it that, was simple. We took the end frame supports from Mother's double bed and laboriously carried the spring base with its angled iron surround down the stairs, knocking lumps of plaster from the walls as it went. Then the heavy bed base was eased with some difficulty into the kitchen and placed about 3ft off the floor, supported at one end on the wooden sideboard and at the other on a wooden chest of drawers. The double mattress was placed underneath the frame, on the floor, and then the whole structure was draped in blankets. We never bothered to undress when we took shelter here, and most of the time even kept our shoes on. Often we were unable to sleep, but just listened, terrified, to the slow whining drum of the German heavy bombers as they flew in the night sky above us. We heard the screeching bombs as they fell through the air and the muffled explosions as they hit their targets in the distant dock areas, or louder explosions if they hit closer to home. The constant rapid crack of the anti-aircraft guns gave us hope and a feeling of comfort, as did the incessant clanging of fire-engine bells.

On one occasion a bomb dropped in Fielding Street, where we were living. It blasted houses on both sides of the street and I remember the house shaking and the coal soot dropping down the chimney into the fire surround. It was difficult to breathe with all the dust and clogging soot filling our mouths and nostrils. The front of the house including the parlour was damaged, all the windows were blown in, curtains ripped to shreds, and the tyres of our precious transport, bicycles, lacerated. I don't remember the brown sticky tape on the windows easing the problem of flying glass, but I suppose we were too close to the impact for it to be of any use. If we had sheltered in the parlour we would no doubt have been severely cut too. On hearing the desperate screams of people on the street outside, Dad immediately left the comparative safety of our shelter and went out into the street to give assistance.

Mother pleaded with him, saying "Be careful, Harold."

"Don't you worry, Peggy love. I'll just see if I can help the neighbours. You stay there and look after the children." The rest of us stayed in our flimsy bunker cuddling together and cowering the night away. It was approaching dawn when the raid was finally over and the all-clear sounded.

Looking at the damage in the morning light, I could see a huge crater in the middle of the street. The fronts of houses were obliterated and the sky was visible through the roof rafters where the slates had vanished. I wondered where the people I knew had gone to. Some were in hospital and others had gone to stay with friends.

Dad had conscientiously gone to work that day even though he had had no real sleep, and so when he returned he was despondent and angry. I remember his worrying words: "We're finished. The docks are useless — dock gates have been blown off, ships sunk and others on their sides in the water. The warehouses are ablaze and shipping too. We're now wide open for the Germans to invade us." These were the sentiments of not just my dad but of thousands of dockworkers who had seen their means of livelihood devastated overnight. The fear of a Nazi invasion was terrifying news to everybody, although thankfully Dad was too old to be called up for active service.

"What would you do, Dad, if the Germans came?" I asked.

"I would join the resistance, son," he replied.

"What is that, Dad?"

"It's a secret underground army that would attack the Germans with stealth."

"Where would you get the guns from, Dad?" I enquired.

"I'm not quite sure, but I think that the Americans would help us," he said.

I never remember my mother being hysterical, even under the most trying and terrifying conditions. She was obviously fearful on many, many, occasions, but she never let her fear be felt by her children. Quite often during an air raid, when Dad was not yet home from work, I would look at Mother and sense the apprehension that emanated from her very being. She would hold me, stroke my head and confide in me with calm and simple sentences:

"I wonder where your Dad is, Bryan? . . . I hope he's all right." Sometimes Dad would have to walk home from the docks during a raid because the trams had stopped. He'd shelter momentarily in shop doorways, not lingering for too long because of his fear for the family. It must have been a blessed relief for him when he finally turned the corner of Fielding Street, sometimes having walked all the way from Gladstone Dock, to see that the house was still intact. I know it was always a relief for Mam and us kids when our steadfast dad walked proudly through that unlocked door.

Air-raid shelters began to be opened up in the basements of suitable buildings. One night we sheltered under an old shop on the other side of Kensington. I always remember this location because of a remark made by my brother Peter. We had spent the long night crowded into a cold and damp basement shelter with lots of other folk, all huddled together on the concrete floor, wrapped up in blankets that we had brought along, and we were making our way home after the all-clear had sounded in the early hours of the morning. He was in his pram being pushed by Mam, while Monica and Gerald and I were walking alongside — Dad was doing fire picket somewhere. Peter must have been two or three years old and he looked up at the clear night sky from a prone position in his pram and said, "Why are all those holes in the blanket, Mam?" Of course he was referring to the stars in the night sky. But his simple child's remark made us all laugh and helped to ease away the fearful terror of the air raid we had just endured. It's amazing that young Peter should think that the sky was a blanket full of holes letting the light shine through, but when you think about it, children in fear do cover themselves with a blanket — I know that I did. If you have ever done this yourself, you will notice that light shines through what appears to be holes but what are in fact the tiny spaces between the weaves of cloth.

We used to try out various air-raid shelters, I cannot remember why, but sometimes the one we were heading for was full up and we would be directed towards another. People got wise to this and started to head for the shelters earlier than was necessary for fear of not getting in at all. One evening, when it was still daylight, we were heading for the shelter in the basement of Rathbone School, which I believe was in Albany Road, when out of the clouds we saw a huge German bomber appear. Mam was pushing the pram as usual, which as well as Peter was loaded with blankets, bottles of drinking water and something to eat. We were about a hundred yards from the shelter entrance. Mam shouted out to us at the top of her voice: "Run, kids, run, hurry up, run!" We did not have to be told twice, and were soon well ahead of her and her speeding pram.

Later in the war a corrugated galvanised-sheet steel shelter was developed, the Anderson shelter, named after the Home Secretary Anthony Anderson. These were allotted to people with gardens. A pit about 30in deep would be dug into the earth, and then the shelter would be bolted together and placed into the pit. Earth would be built up around and over the top of the shelter. The problem with this shelter was that it became a trap for water, but if the raids were bad enough people would dive into them regardless.

Another type of shelter was the iron table, which was placed in the dining room to replace the conventional table. The sides were covered in steel mesh and you slept underneath it. How people were selected for these shelters I do not know, because only a minority of people had them. Nobody had Anderson shelters in the inner city of Liverpool, because nobody had gardens to put them in, so I suppose they were reserved for people in the suburbs who lived close to likely target areas for bombing, or perhaps they were allotted to people with disabilities who could not make it to the main shelters — that seems the most likely. The only person I knew who had a table shelter lived opposite our house. Her name was Mrs MacMenemy. She lived alone with her little husband — they had no children — and a monkey. She invited Mother over to her house to inspect the shelter; of course I went along too — but I was sorry because as I went to stroke the monkey it bit me on the arm. It was the first time that I had ever seen a monkey. Mrs MacMenemy had two spare rooms in her house so she hired them out to Scott's the grocer's who used them as an emergency warehouse for perishable foodstuffs. This of course made sense. With the main warehouses in the port of Liverpool being constantly fire-bombed, retail outlets had resorted to finding their own means of stockpiling vital food supplies. Mrs MacMenemy was also very handy with the needle and thread and made a suit for her husband. Dad used to chuckle quietly at the expense of Mr MacMenemy as he paraded nonchalantly up and down our street in his homemade suit, smoking his briar pipe. Tobacco goods were not rationed but hard to come by. They were never on display in the shops but hidden beneath the counter. The unwritten rule was that cigarettes were for regular customers: if you bought a paper in the shop, then the proprietor would put his hand beneath the counter and bring forth a packet of cigarettes. Mr MacMenemy supplemented his tobacco allowance by collecting used tea-leaves from the pot, which he would dry and mix well into his thick twist tobacco. He'd be as proud as punch striding along in his new suit and puffing away at his pipe, although the mixture of tea and tobacco was inclined to burn abnormally and give off a lot of smoke.

On such occasions, Dad would look at the sky and say, "There's going to be a heavy air raid tonight, son."

"How do you know that, Dad?" I would ask.

"I get my information from watching Mr MacMenemy. Just look at him . . . he's laying down a smokescreen so the bombers can't see the targets."

Mrs MacMenemy came across to our house one day and told Mam that she had spotted her husband stealing fresh tea from the caddy to put into his briar pipe. She was furious with him, and, being twice his size, she let him know about it in no uncertain terms.

I cannot remember exactly when it was, but at some stage brick and concrete shelters began to be built in the streets of Liverpool. We had four in Fielding Street, all in a line on the opposite side of the road to us, on the odd-number side. They were about 40ft long, about 10ft wide and 8ft high, with 9in-thick brick walls and a 4in-thick concrete roof, all built straight onto the road surface. Some time later the wall size was increased to 14in thick, and the roof thickness to 6in. We felt more secure in those shelters because of their rigidity and nearness to home. There was also a concrete emergency water tank positioned at the Kensington end of the row of shelters. This was about 8ft in diameter and about 4ft high. It was kept full of water by the fire department, the only trouble being that in summer it became stagnant and turned bright green and was a breeding ground for aquatic wildlife.

On occasions I was carried from my bed to the shelter during an air raid. I can remember seeing the night sky aglow and bright red with the reflection of the burning fires, and seeing the arc of the searchlights sweeping across the sky. On other occasions I would witness barrage balloons burning fiercely, having been struck by lightning in an electrical thunderstorm, and when this happened the heavy wire cable holding them aloft would crash to the ground causing damage to the roofs of properties and injuring people. Well into the mornings after a raid, when the all-clear had finally sounded, Micky and I would be full of excitement and would go around the streets looking for shrapnel souvenirs. These misshapen and jagged metallic pieces could be from anti-aircraft shells, tracer bullets or aircraft cannon fire and were highly prized possessions. They were exhibited and discussed in great detail at school with the other kids — especially if you found a piece with flesh and blood on it. We used to use the smaller pieces as you would marbles: the first boy would throw a piece of shrapnel in front of him, then the second boy would throw a piece and try to get as near as possible to the first, and provided he could span both pieces between his thumb and little finger he was deemed to have won and took the prize. We had no marbles, so our trouser pockets were always full of shrapnel and because of its jagged nature it tore our pockets to shreds and also cut our thighs. Our world was an adventure playground. We were forever exploring bombed-out buildings, never going directly to school but always via a string of derelict buildings. Follow the leader was the most popular game. The most adventurous went in front, followed by a line of lesser heroes, descending in order of character with tail-end Charlie the weakest of the gang. I was never the leader but then I was never tail-end Charlie either.

Monica and Gerald were temporarily evacuated to North Wales along with thousands of other children. I refused to go because I was a clinger to my mother. They went by train, with a brown parcel label pinned to their jackets indicating who they were. The idea was to take them away from the industrial and dockland danger zones.

Mam would receive her housekeeping money from Dad on Saturday afternoon, when Dad got paid. By this time we had eaten most of our rations. Mam would go shopping for her meat ration allowance, which she always saved until the Saturday so that we could have a roast dinner on the Sunday. She would also buy plenty of potatoes, carrots, swedes, onions and cabbage — vegetables which we ate plenty of were not rationed. Monica usually went with Mam to help carry the heavy root vegetables, and sometimes took the old pram. I would be given the ration books and some money and told to go to Scott's, the grocer.

"Here you are, son," Mam would say. "Now you ask Mr Shallicker nicely if you can have some of next week's rations and don't be rude to him." She said this because on occasions I suppose I had been rude. I was young and impressionable, and if people said something to me I accepted it without thinking.

Once Dad gave me some money and said, "Now go down to Scott's, Bryan, and ask Mr Shallicker for some broken biscuits and if he says he hasn't got any then ask him to break a few for me." I did exactly as I was told: I did not see any harm in it but I do remember a huge friendly grin spreading across Mr Shallicker's cheerfully happy face.

"Who sent you along, young Kelly?" he asked.

"Me Dad did, Mr Shallicker," I replied.

"Well, here you are then, son," he said, handing me a brown paper bag. "You tell your Dad that he is very very lucky because I spilled a tin of biscuits on the shop floor this morning and before I could pick them up the delivery man walked all over them and broke them into pieces with his big boots."

I always tried to catch the attention of Mr Shallicker when I entered the shop — I didn't want to be served by his assistant and suffer a rebuff because Mam would be mad at me, and had specifically told me to go to Mr Shallicker. He was a kindly man, and I managed to catch his eye. He knew we were a big family and I don't ever remember him refusing my mother's request.

"What do you want now, young fella?" he enquired.

"Me Mam said could she have some food off the next week's ration?"

"Have you got your ration books?" he asked.

"Yiss, Mr Shallicker," I said, handing over the well-thumbed and grubby books. "What does your mother want?" he said.

"Margarine, tea, sugar and some bacon for me dad's breakfast."

"You realise that you will not have any rations next week, don't you?" he reminded me.

"Yiss, Mr Shallicker," I responded. The kindly grocer adjusted the ration books, handed the groceries and the books back to me and said, "That will be five and nine pence halfpenny." I gave him a ten bob note and received four and twopence halfpenny change. "Now put that money in your pocket. We don't want you coming back here saying you were given the wrong change do we?"

"No, Mr Shallicker. Thank you, Mr Shallicker." I beamed at him and left the shop.

CHAPTER
EIGHT

Senior School

Sacred Heart of Jesus Roman Catholic School was situated on Mount Vernon, a high point in Liverpool; it was a boys' school. Gary Taylor, the headmaster, would cycle to school each day on his sit-up-and-beg BSA bicycle. He'd take off his cycling clips, put his bike safely away, then take the school parade. He was a small man approaching retirement years, and I should think from his bearing that he was an old soldier and had possibly served in the First World War.

All the kids ran about wildly and shouted as kids do. If one lad was eating a cooking apple — as was the norm, because I don't remember any other type of apples during the war years — there would be a crowd of others around him begging for a bite. "I claim the core!" one would say.

"Two's up on the core!" would claim another.

"Three's up!" would come the shouts of others.

Mr Taylor would blow his whistle and immediately everybody would stop running about and stand rigidly still where they stood. Complete silence would reign, only to be broken by a second shrill blast from Mr Taylor's whistle. Then everybody would walk to their allotted positions, class by class, and would line up standing stiffly to attention in two ranks. On the third blast of the whistle we would raise our right arms and touch the shoulder of the person to our right. We would then shuffle along to the left with our arms still outstretched and still touching the person on our right. On the next blast of the whistle we would drop our right arm to our side — this was known as right dressing. Mr Taylor would then stride along the ranks of pupils like a commanding officer inspecting his troops. Scrawny, bedraggled, unkempt, scruffy, dirty, tattered and very hungry — we were always very hungry. Mr Taylor was always immaculately dressed in a pinstriped lounge suit, with clean white shirt and smart tie, and his shoes were always highly polished. In our eyes he was a picture of sartorial elegance. Sometimes he would look at us rather quizzically, well aware of the deprivations that we and our parents were suffering because of this terrible war. But nevertheless this was a school, an institute of education and learning, and standards of dress, cleanliness and morals must not be allowed to drop no matter what the reason. Mr Taylor halted momentarily in front of one of the worse specimens of scarecrowism, looking the boy over from head to toe before asking the quaking lad: "Why have you not polished your boots this morning, boy?"

"Me Mam's got no polish, Zir," was the boy's immediate answer.

"Yes, I can understand that, but you must try and do something about your boots in future, do you understand me?"

We all wore short trousers and ankle boots. The boots were unpolishable because the highly lustrous black coating was worn away to reveal a scarred and uneven surface of mostly grey leather. This was the result of our young and adventurous lifestyle of shinning up and down brick walls on our way to and from school, and kicking empty bean cans about the streets because we had no balls to play with.

Mr Taylor would continue his inspection of his weary troops and continue with admonishments: "Why are your knees and your neck dirty, boy — didn't you wash this morning?"

"No, Zir."

"In Heaven's name why not?" exclaimed a furious Mr Taylor.

"Me Mam's got no soap, Zir."

"But you could have washed without soap."

"We've got no water eeder, Zir. The water pipe's been bombed." After the forlorn pupil inspection was completed the final whistle blast was heard and the ranks of children turned either to the left or to the right. This was determined by memory training so that the ranks followed each other like a long winding snake into the womb of the school.

CHAPTER
NINE

Religious Instruction

The school was of Victorian vintage with very high ceilings and tall window frames containing small panes of glass, and heavy wood and glass partitions separating the classrooms. We were seated two to a desk on benches that were attached to the desk. On the top of the desk were two drilled holes into which earthenware inkpots rested, and under the hinged lids we kept our exercise books. Every Monday morning after the school attendance register had been completed, there came the Mass attendance register. The school register kept tabs on our attendance at school and the Mass register kept track of our religious devotions over the preceding weekend. In my unblinkered view I firmly believed that religious instruction took precedence over normal education or the three Rs as they were known, reading, 'riting and 'rithmetic. As part of our religious instruction we were obliged to go to confession on a Friday evening and receive absolution for our sins. We were then required to go to Mass on Sunday morning, and during the Mass receive the body of Christ. On Sunday evening there was Sunday school or Benediction. The teacher would commence the Mass register by calling out the names of the boys one by one, a ritual that I and others always dreaded.

On hearing his name, Jones would stand up in the aisle in trepidation and proceed to tell the teacher of his devotions over the weekend.

"Cunfession —"; his well rehearsed list of obligations was interrupted by the teacher's stern and commanding voice.

"Speak up clearly and talk slowly, Jones!"

Jones continued his phraseology: "Cunfession, Mass, 'Oly Cummunion, Benediction, Zir." Jones would now take his seat.

"White."

"Cunfession, Mass, 'Oly Cummunion, Zir."

"Why did you not go to Benediction, White?"

"I had to go to my sick a'nts with me Mam, Zir."

"Where does your aunt live?"

"Bootle, Zir."

"Isn't there a church near your aunt's?"

"I don't know, Zir."

"Well, you should find out in future. Now sit down."

"Kelly."

"Cunfession, Mass, 'Oly Cummunion, Benediction, Zir." At this point one of the priests from the local church, the Sacred Heart of Jesus, happened to enter the classroom. A stern and sour-faced priest whom none of the boys liked, he brought with him an aura of fear and uneasiness.

"What time did you go to Mass, boy?"

"Ten o'clock, Farder."

"Who said the Mass, boy?"

"Errrm, Farder Danna, Farder."

"Are you sure of that, boy?"

"Errrm yiss, Farder."

"Sit down, boy." I sat down nervously but gratefully. The teacher continued going through the ritualistic register and the priest would continue with his interrogative interruptions. I silently sat there very pleased with myself as I appeared to have beaten the system — I must surely have guessed the correct name of the priest taking the ten o'clock Mass.

The catechism was one of the most important books that we were all obliged to purchase from the church. It was a questionnaire with answers on the doctrines and principles of Roman Catholicism, and had to be studied each day, the answers memorised and answered in parrot fashion when asked by the teacher or priest or indeed other boys in the class. After catechism study was over the teacher would say, "Put your catechisms away, children." Then he would question us one by one to check our absorption of its contents. On some occasions he would divide the class into two sections with a boy from one section asking a boy from the other section a relevant question, and this would have to be performed from memory.

"Who made you?"

"God made me."

"Why did God make you?"

"God made me to love him and obey him in this world and to be happy with him forever in the next."

"In what image did God make you?"

"God made me in his own image."

This question and answer exercise would go on for about half an hour with frequent interruptions by the teacher to put right the stumbling and hesitant answers of most of the boys. "You will all take your catechisms home tonight and study them. Father O'Toole will be questioning you on your catechism tomorrow and I don't want a repetition of today's very bad answers."

CHAPTER
TEN

First Confession

We were taught how to make our confessions, how to follow Mass, and how to receive Holy Communion, how to bless ourselves by dipping clean fingers in the holy water font and performing the sign of the cross. Our first confession and our first Holy Communion were important milestones for us in the eyes of the Church.

On the appointed day we assembled in the playground and were marched regimentedly to the church, which backed onto the school in Hall Lane. Via the rear entrance, we ascended a huge flight of stone steps, then meekly and very quietly entered the house of God, all the time shepherded by frowning, gesticulating teachers. We blessed ourselves, momentarily knelt when facing the altar, following the teacher's every movement as he led the way. When we came to a line of confessional boxes, we filed into the wooden pews that stood either side of them, and one by one we entered the confessional. The priest who was taking the confessions had his name displayed outside the box, and we had no choice in this selection.

I was to be administered by Father Doyle, an old and cantankerous Irish priest who was long set in his rigid ways. As boys came out of the confessional we moved up on the long pew, three to go, two to go, one to go — my turn next. I meekly entered the small enclosure with a certain amount of trepidation. It was dark and it had a smell all of its own, quite different from any smell I had ever encountered, neither registering as pleasant or unpleasant. The priest was partly hidden behind a screen built into a partition of the box. He was sitting side on to the screen, which had a thin curtain pulled across it so that I could barely make out the outlines of his face. I knelt on a padded knee-rest, blessed myself and said in a meek and subdued voice — inaudible to those waiting their turn outside the box, I hoped, but just audible to the priest — "Pray, Farder, give me your blessing for I have sinned."

"Tell me of your sins, my child," the demanding voice boomed from the other side of the screen.

"I have disobeyed my Mudder three times and my Farder once. I have missed Mass and Holy Cummunion once." Here I paused in contemplation.

"Anything else?" said the priest.

"And I have stolen three biscuits from my Mudder's biscuit tin." To me this was the worst sin of all: there was a war on and I had stolen rations that did not belong to me.

"You know that it is a mortal sin on your soul to miss Mass and Holy Communion, don't you, my child?"

"Yiss, Farder."

"Then why did you do it?"

"I was sick, Farder."

"That is no excuse. Do you realise that if you were to die with a mortal sin on your soul, then your spirit would be damned forever to the burning fires of hell and damnation?"

"Yiss, Farder."

"I want you to promise that you will not miss Mass again, is that clear?"

"I promise, Farder."

"I now absolve thee from thy sins in the name of the Father, the Son and the Holy Ghost." said Father Doyle. "And your penance shall be ten Our Fathers and ten Hail Marys, and may the Blessing of God be with you."

I left the confines of that stuffy box and brushed past the next lad as he entered. It seemed that I had been in there a long time but it was probably only a few minutes. I made my way to the altar rails, genuflecting and blessing myself at every turn, then I knelt down and did my penance of ten Our Fathers and ten Hail Marys as fast as I could because I knew that other people assessed your sinning by the length of time you spent at the altar rails saying your penance. It was late afternoon now and the teachers had presumably gone home, no doubt confident that they had performed their religious educational duty for the week. I left the church by the front entrance, performing a continuous series of self-blessings and genuflections with a final font-dipping as I left. What a wonderful feeling of relief, free from the constraints of my religion, free in the knowledge that if I were to die now I would ascend immediately to Heaven! As I made my final exit from the long passageway leading from the main body of the church I saw daylight, felt fresh air and had an overwhelming feeling of freedom. But how could priests live a life like that, I thought? Why don't old people laugh or even smile? What a dull place for God to live in. Why doesn't God stop the war?

I remember the parish priest visiting our modest home each Sunday afternoon. On occasions we children would warn each other that he was on his way. "The preest's kumming, Bry," would be the warning shout from Monica, and with this knowledge I would hide myself from his all-pervading presence. On the many times I was not quick enough to give him the slip I would have to endure his interrogation. He would enquire who had been to Mass and who had received the Holy Sacrament. We were all fearful of him, even our poor mother, who would be admonished if she was silly enough to say she had not been to Mass. After her reprimand she would reach for the mantleshelf and take down half a crown and hand it to the priest — a priest of the Holy Roman Catholic Church, a rich international organisation, presumably collecting money for the poor. The priests were always well dressed, and well shod, with polished shoes, nice trilby hats and fine black heavy overcoats. They were never thin or hungry-looking, but with faces and bodies well padded out they expressed a dominant attitude, and most people appeared to be afraid of them. It seemed to me that they were robbing the poor in a subtle way to hand over to the rich. I knew instinctively that my mother could not afford to give money away like that. Couldn't these agents of God realise that it was we who were poor, or didn't they care? They may have spoken a lot of fine words, but to me they never seemed to show any real compassion, which was quite evident when they confronted my poor mother and her hungry brood. It was these experiences in my early life that turned me away from organised religion of any type, and especially Roman Catholicism and its priests. When I see Catholics and Protestants, Muslims and Jews, Hindus and Sikhs and hundreds of other religiously committed peoples killing each other over religious principles instead of embracing each other with human principles, then I firmly believe that innocent babies should not be entered into any religion before they have the strength to say no. This world would be a happier place if the United Nations, instead of spending millions of pounds in its attempts to stop wars between nations feuding mainly over religious problems, strived for international agreement on the curtailing of religious indoctrination of innocent infants that turns them into the puppets of religious dogma. At eighteen years of age, when youth has gained manhood or womanhood, young people are well able to reason for themselves: this is time enough for them to decide if religion is to be part of their lives.

CHAPTER
ELEVEN

First Holy Communion

My first Holy Communion took place on the Sunday following my first confession, which was on the Friday. Mother spent a lot of time sprucing me up as best she could, then Father took me along to the Mass. There were a lot of other spruced-up boys there, and also girls, who were wearing white ankle-length dresses with white headdresses and face veils, which must have cost their parents a fortune. I suppose the girls were going to be symbolically married to Christ, although we were just innocent children performing the next phase of our mandatory religious indoctrination. I am not aware of how many children enjoyed what was happening to them, but I certainly did not: I merely accepted meekly because I did not know how not to and because I loved my parents and would not rebel against them.

Dad was a churchgoer because he was brought up from childhood to believe in Christianity and Roman Catholicism. He could just as well have ended up a Protestant, a Jew, a Muslim, a Hindu, or any of the other countless religions that do their best to indoctrinate and mould young innocent children.

Grandmother Kelly's house was cluttered with religious icons, on mantleshelves and ledges, on walls and even on the backs of doors. Why? Because she herself was indoctrinated from the cradle.

I followed Dad into church and copied his every move and gesture, font-dipping, blessing, genuflection, sitting down, standing up, kneeling down, standing up then sitting down again. It seemed to go on forever, the priest and his assistants and altar boys would make their way to the high altar to begin the Mass. As an observer I did admire the solemn ritual of the Mass, its pomp and its pageantry, but I did not want to be part of it. The priest conducted the service in Latin, a foreign language that most people did not understand, incense burned, hand bells rang and people murmured guiltily to themselves, "Through my fault, through my fault, through my most grievous fault", at the same time tapping their abdomens with their right hands. The gates in the centre of the altar rails were then closed and a white cloth that hung from the other side of the rails was draped across them. The priest opened a beautiful casket that lay on the altar and from it he drew a chalice of red wine. He raised the chalice with both hands and with magical words changed it into the blood of Jesus Christ, which he then proceeded to drink. After this he drew from the casket a plate of unleavened bread, and with more magic transformed it into the body of Christ. At this point we made our way to the altar rails, knelt down and clasped our hands together and rested our elbows on the white cloth. The priest and his assistants now went along the line of kneeling worshippers and placed the holy sacrament onto their protruding tongues. After receiving the body of Christ I stood up and left the altar rails with head bowed, eyes to the floor and hands clasped. On reaching my pew I genuflected, blessed myself and resumed my kneeling position until the body of Christ was absorbed into my being. The rest of the Mass was taken up by prayers and sermons from the pulpit. We were asked to pray for servicemen killed, wounded and missing in action, and some individual names were read out for special prayers.

The church was always packed during the war years with civilians and service personnel alike. There were also remnants of the Free French, Free Dutch and representatives of other European nations that had been overrun by the Nazis, and these servicemen were mostly in naval uniform — Liverpool, as a major sea port, was home to many foreign ships and their crews. But it was always a relief for me when the priest saying the Mass and his retinue of assistants and altar boys carrying their religious paraphernalia made their way to the vestry.

I spent a good deal of my time during the Mass gazing at the huge window at the rear of the altar and marvelling at the intricacy and beauty of its stained-glass pictures. I would watch the rays of the sun as they shone across the myriad colours of the glass and dwell in a self-imposed trance. I wanted to be out there in that sunshine: I was a young boy with thin blood racing through my uncluttered arteries; I didn't want to be locked away in this beautiful church with its congregation of devout worshippers and constantly coughing pensioners.

CHAPTER
TWELVE

Bed Bugs

The main trouble with the house at 20 Fielding Street was the infestation of cockroaches and especially bed bugs. Cucumber peelings used to be put down to kill the cockroaches, but bed bugs were a different matter. We had these for as long as I can remember and that was well into my teenage years; in fact I don't think we ever got rid of them completely, just kept them down to manageable proportions. The horrible little creatures would hide and multiply in any crack or crevice they could find but mostly in the bed springs and mattress seams so that they could be as near to their host as possible, just a short crawling distance away. But when accommodation in those areas was full to capacity they would board themselves in the suburbs, such as the folds of wallpaper. Wallpaper was inclined to peel because the houses were damp and bugs would nest behind the peeled paper and breed. When I spotted a likely breeding place I would rub my hand against the paper and apply pressure: if there was a distinct crackle I knew I had hit the target; this would be confirmed by the presence of blood protruding from the bulge. Bugs would also breed behind the skirting boards, in the panelling of doors, behind architraves, in the cracks and joints of furniture or in the hessian bindings of books. From these suburban retreats they would commute to the bed chamber when they knew it was occupied by an unsuspecting host. Their keen sense of smell would send them on nightly predatory missions. These dreadful nocturnal blood-sucking parasites were my number one enemy. On wakening in the mornings I would find spots of blood splattering the bed sheet and the remains of bugs that had been killed by my fitful tossing and turning throughout the night. This awful vision was always the signal for me to attack the enemy, which I did on a very regular basis. I would strip the bedding and mattress from the bed frame, then with an inch of lighted candle stuck to the end of a wooden stick attack their strongholds in the bed springs. There would be a nauseating smell as I fire-bombed them, and the ones that were bloated with my blood would explode with a definite crack. I killed tens of thousands, but they multiplied as fast as I could annihilate them. I am convinced that most terraced houses were infested with this evil, so no matter what you did to ease the problem the ugly brown creatures would migrate along the terrace houses through minuscule cracks in walls and ceilings via the floor or roof spaces. I'm not quite sure if the local government authority had a department to deal with this type of infestation, as they did with rats and mice, but if they had, would the general public use it? People are loath to admit they are plagued by such horrible creatures, being a taboo subject outside the family, and conjuring up feelings of guilt. Bed bugs could be imported into a clean home through infested second-hand furniture, or even second-hand books. I don't know if the problem has disappeared in this modern world, but do people still keep it quietly to themselves?

Dad and Mam tried to improve the old house by decorating all the rooms. The front room was hardly ever used: it was the parlour kept for best, so to speak, in case we had important visitors. We had the old gas lighting removed and electric lights installed, which made a big difference. I'll always remember that we never had shades on the lights, just the bare bulbs, because we could not afford shades — shades were for posh people. We also had a gas cooker installed in the back kitchen, which improved Mother's culinary expertise since she was not now reliant on the open fire. Dad also whitewashed the brick walls surrounding the back yard. He bought quicklime in lumps, placed it in a galvanised bucket together with a couple of candles then added cold water. After a very short time there was a chemical reaction, the water boiled and the candles melted, and the lime was reduced to a white milky substance called limewash. This limewash was painted onto the brick walls in the yard and the outside lavatory, and when it dried it was so brilliant it hurt your eyes. The candles helped to put a glossy sheen on its surface so that when the sun's rays reflected off it, the inside of the house became much brighter.

CHAPTER THIRTEEN

Mother & Father

Mother ate very little. She was quite a small woman, about 5ft 2in in height, and very slim. Her preoccupation in life was her husband and her children. They were the first to be fed at the dining table; she came last. I always admired my mother for her quality of motherhood, and I admire women in general because of the experiences I gained from understanding my own mother. She would go short of food during the war so that her children didn't go hungry.

Dad got paid on a Saturday at lunch time when he finished work — in those days everybody worked a minimum five and a half day week. He would come straight home and give Mam her housekeeping money. She would then give me five shillings and select a pawn ticket after thumbing through a wad of them.

"I think that's the one, Bryan," she would say before telling me to get Dad's best suit and best boots out of Joe Furlong's the pawnbroker's shop on the corner of Kemble Street and Kensington. She would then place the rent money on the mantleshelf together with some half-crowns for various eventualities. Having catered for the major bills she would then go shopping for food, with her little purse tucked into her coat pocket and her silver shopping bag made from barrage balloon material over her arm, the ration books secure inside it. Underneath an old brown coat she wore a pinafore over her polka-dot dress and on her head she wore a turban to hide her curlers. The turban was made from a length of odd curtain material, and was knotted at the front.

Saturday afternoon was Dad's time to relax, that is if he was not doing overtime or on night shift. The dockers were well organised within a trade union, the Transport and General Workers Union. Over the years they had negotiated good working conditions for themselves and were continually improving on them. They operated what is termed a closed shop, in other words, if you did not have a union card then you had no chance of getting into the dock system. They stood by each other and if they thought one of their work mates was being badly treated or victimised, they would stand together to the point of withdrawing their labour. I've lost count of the times when Dad would come home and tell Mam that he was on strike along with thousands of others; it meant that times were leaner still when that happened. Sometimes there were strike rallies, demonstrations and marches, and if it was a big issue it would spread to other ports throughout Britain and even overseas: international solidarity was the order of the day. Working Saturday night was known to the dockers as the golden nugget — with good reason, as they got paid treble time for it.

But Saturday afternoon relaxing in front of the open coal fire, reading the *Liverpool Echo*, listening to a match and picking a couple of horses was heaven to Dad. When he had selected a few likely winners he would scribble them on a piece of paper with an indelible pencil. He never added his name but applied a *nom de plume* to identify himself in case he won. There were no betting shops in those days and it was illegal to bet unless you were on a race course, so the ordinary working man, who could not afford to visit a race course, had no alternative but to break the rules of society in order to have a flutter. Dad would give me the stake money and betting slip and then I would be off down the street to find the bookie's runner. He was the man who hung around the street corners, collected the bets and then took them to the bookie. No questions were asked: you just slid the betting slip and money into his hand and melted away, making sure that an officer of the law was not in range.

Mam would come back from shopping and prepare the evening meal while Dad would listen to the football results on the wireless. He would then check his football coupon and throw it on the fire in disgust,

"Ha, well!" he would exclaim. "Perhaps the horses can do better." He didn't gamble, it was just a little flutter, and it helped him build up hope and dream of a brighter future for the family. After tea Dad would have a shave and wash down in the back kitchen sink, then go down the yard to the outdoor lavatory. Meanwhile, Mam would clean up the tea dishes with Monica and me grudgingly helping her, then take the rollers from her hair, have a quick wash, and go upstairs to put on her best dress. This was to be her big night out. She would come downstairs smiling, with a little make-up on her face. "Where is your Dad?" she would ask.

"He's down the yard, Mam," Monica would say.

"I suppose he's fallen asleep after his dinner," she would say. "Bryan, go down and wake him up, there's a good lad, and tell him I'm ready."

Dad and Mam went out most Saturday nights, usually to one of the local public houses, Gleesons on the corner of Seldon Street and Romilly Street, the Royal Arch on the corner of our street and Kensington, or the Sefton Arms on the Kensington corner of Seldon Street. Whichever it was it was no more than five minutes' walking distance, and the public houses all closed at ten o'clock — and there was no drinking-up time either. The women, all neighbours, would mostly sit together jangling, while the men gathered around the dart board; most pubs had dart teams and were in local leagues. Darts were taken very seriously and it was a big occasion when a match was on. Dad liked a game of darts and was quite good at it, and was a well-respected member of the Gleesons darts team. There was no form of music other than the wireless in pubs but sometimes a gramophone would be wound up and old records played. Then the regulars would break into song. Dad liked a pint of bitter and Mam would drink a Mackeson. A couple of hours in the pub made a different woman out of her: she would come home with Dad and they would be quite merry. I can never remember Mam and Dad ever falling out or arguing because they were quite closely bonded to each other.

If Dad was not working the weekend he would take Monica and me to church on the Sunday morning. Mother never went to church as she was too busy in the house. She was a good woman but not religious, and although she never mentioned religion, she was fearful of the church hierarchy. Monday morning saw Dad's best boots and best suit back into the pawn shop, with, of course, Dad's consent. Dad would always joke about this arrangement. "The suit is better off in Joe Furlong's anyway. We haven't got a wardrobe here to put it in." Mam would always warn me to be very careful that nobody saw me going into Joe Furlong's shop, as pawning was a social stigma that she did not wish to carry.

"Go the back way, Bryan," she would tell me. I did as I was told, walked down the back yard, out of the gate, then up the jigger, across Seldon Street, up Seldon Street jigger into Kemble Street, then a quick dash when nobody was looking and into the redemption part of the shop. If I was lucky there would be no customers; if I was not there would sometimes be a queue of people, especially on Monday morning. Some in the queue actually knew each other but they would never speak, pretending that they had not seen one another. Most people had brown paper parcels under their arms, which the pawnbroker would open and check.

"How much, Mrs Ball?"

"Six shillings, Joe," she would say, hopefully.

"Five bob," would be his quick reply.

"OK then, Joe," she would answer. Those behind Mrs Ball could see exactly what she was pawning, and of course those behind the next customer would have a preview of their offerings, but nothing would be said while in the shop — it was all good information for jangling about later on. Joe would rewrap Mrs Ball's bundle, pin a label to it then pass the bundle to a young lad assistant for stowing away.

"Here you are, Mrs Ball," he would say, passing over to her the redemption part of the ticket together with two half-crowns.

"Thanks, Joe," she would murmur, and leave the shop. The next woman would move towards the opening in the security grill across the counter.

"Morning, Mrs Poppitt. Curtains again, is it?"

"Yes, Joe," she would respond.

Opening the bundle Joe would ask, "How much?"

"Five shillings please".

"Sorry, there's not much call for curtains and these are showing their age. I'll give you two and six."

"Can't you make it three bob, Joe?" she would plead.

Joe relented. "OK, but just this once."

"Thanks, Joe," and she would leave the shop.

"What have you got there, young Kelly? Dad's suit?"

"Yiss, Mr Furlong." Mam had primed me on good manners when talking to Joe.

"How much, five bob?" He asked the question then answered it himself in rapid fire while checking the goods on offer. He wrapped them up again and put them into the system. "Here you are, young fella me lad," passing me a ticket and two half-crowns. "Now hold that money tight and run straight home."

"Thanks, Mr Furlong," I responded and hurriedly left his shop. Jewellery was a commodity that was often offered to the pawnbroker, but these items were usually the last things to be pawned. Women in dire straits would often pawn their wedding ring; it was very sad when this had to happen. If they could not redeem the ring after the allotted time in pawn it would be put up for sale and displayed in the pawnbroker's front window. The only thing a woman could do in these circumstances was to gaze at her token of love and marriage, dream of what had been and weep gently to herself. These situations had been witnessed in the past by other observant wives and mothers who would read the situation and knowingly understand.

Pawnbrokers perform a social service in times of need. They make a profit from it, but that is the way of the capitalist system. They are human and have feelings like all normal beings, and if they are castigated by some, what would happen if we did not have pawnbrokers, I ask? They will take anything that is saleable, even furniture — their salesrooms are in effect a first class second-hand shop.

"Here you are, Mam, five bob."

"Where is the ticket, Bryan?"

"Oh! Here it is."

"You're going to lose things putting them in your trouser pockets. They're always full of holes — take them off and I'll sew them up. Did you see any one?"

"Only Mrs Ball and Mrs Poppitt."

"Did they say anything to you?"

"No, Mam."

79

"Good," she would say.

Dad's boots would go for pawn later in the week, which is one reason he kept them in tip-top condition, so they would be an attractive item to the pawnbroker. Dad's lack of wealth didn't undermine his personal pride though. He would always look his best when he went to church on Sunday or took his lady out on a Saturday night — boots highly polished, shirt and tie with starched collar suit pressed, no creases, except those in his trousers that you could cut the proverbial butter with, and it was all topped by a smart trilby hat at just the right jaunty angle perched proudly upon his handsome head. He would stroll nonchalantly down the street tall and erect and with his dainty little queen cradling closely and snugly upon his strong muscular arm.

Mother often had to make a calculated decision when one of her brood was ill. Should she go for Dr Bracey? Is the child really ill, or is it something that will pass over? In those days you had to pay five shillings for the doctor to call to your home. More half-crowns would be proffered from the sparse reserves on the mantleshelf, but a wrong decision by mother and she could pay with the life of her child. My heartfelt thanks go to the Labour government with Clement Attlee at its helm and Aneurin Bevin as Minister of Health, which after the war was over in 1945 gained office with a landslide victory. The National Health Service it introduced was and still is a most wonderful and caring institution. I was only a scruffy and impoverished kid of fourteen but I remember it well, and I recall the relief and gratitude of the common British proletariat. It is a well-known fact that the Labour parliament didn't quite get their sums right, but its heart was in the right place. Perhaps they did go over the top with the health service providing for all our medical needs free of charge. But when you consider what was spent over six years of war in arms and ammunition to defend our Empire and our country and indeed the civilised world from the tyrannical oppression of dictatorial rule, then the National Health Service was a move in the right direction.

CHAPTER
FOURTEEN

Laundry

Washing clothes was a major task for women in the pre-war era, yet in the modern world it is so amazingly simple. Mother would try to book a washing-machine, of which there were a limited number in the local washhouse, which was part of the local bath house, where we bathed luxuriously once a week. If Mother could not get a machine she would have to book a stall, which meant that every item of her laundry had to be washed by hand. This was really hard work: the badly soiled items would be scrubbed with a hard scrubbing brush and equally hard soap. On washing day Mother and I would be up early. She always booked as early as possible so that when she brought the clean laundry home it had the maximum time to dry. I would help her push the big old rickety perambulator, our only means of transport apart from old bicycles, which were kept roadworthy by Dad's mechanical know-how. The pram would be loaded high with pillowcases packed with dirty clothing and bed linen. At seven in the morning Mother and I would push the laden pram along the pavements of Kensington towards the corporation washhouse, which was situated at the bottom of Solomon Street, a cul-de-sac. The area around the washhouse would be cluttered with old prams and hand carts and home-made mobility contraptions. Some women were just arriving and others were already there; some were on their own; others had children with them. Those on their own took a chance and left their precious transport in the street outside: some were locked with chains to fixtures like lampposts or drainpipes, others were tied up with bits of rope around their wheels. The women fortunate enough to have someone with them took no chances and arranged to have their transport taken home, with instructions to return it at a specified time, as was the case with Mother. Saturday morning was the ideal time to go to the corporation laundry because it meant that one of Mother's brood would be available to help her; but it was not always possible to book in then. So when it fell in a weekday my schooling would suffer in order that Mother's laundry did not. Mother would be extremely angry if one of us failed to keep to the appointed time. Of course, as kids we did not fully appreciate the enormous pressures that a mother has to bear. If Mother had a machine the laundry would be done in a hour and a half and it would be nice and warm, having been in a clothes dryer. Alternatively, if she had a stall, it would take up to three hours, depending of course on the quantity of laundry.

On completion of her weekly washing Mother would load up our personal transport with pillowslips full of fresh laundry — warm and sweet smelling. She would look exhausted and washed out, and now we had the long trek home, pushing the pram about a mile and a half. Mother's legs were gently bowed, and I used to think it was because of all the carrying that she had had to endure. It was imperative that we got home as quickly as possible because Mother had a myriad of things to accomplish once she got there. The priority was getting the laundry dry, especially the bedding, then doing the shopping, then making the evening meal. Mother was always in top gear no matter what she did — she was always trying to catch up with herself, then to get in front of herself. She had a lifetime's unfulfilled ambition just to get in front of her domestic duties, and as the day wore on she would make little remarks to me such as, "Well now, I have got that out of the way, which means I won't have to do it tomorrow." She was always putting filthy things to soak in buckets of bleach, or peeling the potatoes and carrots for tomorrow's evening dinner and remarking with satisfaction: "Oh! I'm glad that's done, that's saved me a job." But it hadn't really, it just satisfied her impossible ambition. An element of drama was sometimes added to this weekly saga, especially if it rained. Then the laundry would get wet and gain in weight over the mile and a half journey home. The perambulator was known as a double pram, designed for twins, with two collapsible hoods, one at each end, but with the amount of washing Mother had it was impossible to make use of them. On one occasion, about halfway home and while crossing the main Kensington road we had a bit of an accident. The road surface was composed of square stone sets made of hard granite. This made for a very bumpy ride, and while negotiating the tramcar lines at an angle of about forty-five degrees the juddering and vibration was just too much for the old pram, resulting in the complete collapse of one of its wheels and the end of its illustrious domestic career. Without warning the top-heavy pram lurched to its port side and half its precious cargo of warm, clean and fresh-smelling laundry ended up in the middle of a wet, muddy and oil-soaked road before Mother and I had a chance to take preventative measures. Seeing our plight, a complete stranger ran into the centre of the carriageway and helped Mother to bring the pram onto an even keel and then shepherded it to the pavement's edge. I was told to stay next to the bags of laundry as they lay straddling the tramlines; fortunately there were no trams heading for me. Mam struggled to keep the pram upright on the pavement and the Good Samaritan picked up the now quite soiled bags of laundry and carried them to the kerbside. There he kindly reloaded the cargo back onto the top deck of the unsteady pram.

"How far have you got to go, luv?" he asked.

"Oh! Not far!" responded Mother in a nervous and dismissive way.

"Do you think you will manage?" said the Samaritan.

"Yes," said Mother, "and thank you very much for your help."

"You keep the pram on an even keel," the man said. "And you do the pushing, young man." The man continued his journey in the opposite direction to ours but kept looking back towards us.

"Shall I ask him to help us, Mam, 'cos the pram's heavy and he's looking back at us," I asked.

"No!" scolded Mother, "and stop looking at him. We'll be all right," she said to me. The wheel, or what was left of it, was still attached to the pram's axle but instead of being circular it was elliptical. We still had some distance to travel and the hardest part of it was negotiating on and off the kerbs as we crossed roads at right angles to our chosen route. We did finally dock at our berth, 20 Fielding Street, via the back entry. Mother was visibly annoyed with the circumstances but proceeded to continue with her seemingly endless tasks. Some of this wet clothing was hoisted aloft on the high-level back kitchen clothes-horse, while some was loaded onto a low-level clothes-horse, and more still was hung on the metal fire-guard in front of the open coal fire to dry, and some draped from a brass rail that hung beneath the mantleshelf. The rest was placed across chairs, the tops of doors, both downstairs and upstairs — it had to be dried!

"Get some coal on that fire, Bryan, and watch that you don't dirty anything, and when you have done that fill the coal-scuttle again, and chop a few sticks for tomorrow's fire, then bring them in to dry . . . That's a good boy." The now unserviceable transport was stabled in the back yard awaiting the mechanical know-how of our industrious father on his return home from his hard day's labour.

CHAPTER
FIFTEEN

Dad's Morning Ritual

Some of my earliest recollections are of reclining in my bug-infested bed beneath grotty old blankets and an ex-army overcoat. I was conscious of the blood-sucking parasites that infested my bed and used my body as a free-for-all supermarket. It was six o'clock in the morning. I had been awakened by the sounds of what my father referred to as the first tram as it rattled, squeaked and grated its way along the shiny iron tram tracks of Kensington. The trams were powered by electricity from overhead power cables and the electricity was picked up by the trams' trolley and fed into its motors. The motors themselves were comparatively quiet and gave a pleasing sound to the ear. Occasional flashes of light and sparks would emanate from the trolley when it made contact with an insulated supporting junction on its journey down the cable.

From its starting point at the Old Swan tram sheds to its destination point at the Pier Head terminus, the tramcar would pick up early-morning workers at every stop. These were mainly dockers, or men associated with the docks — women would not be among them, nor office workers, as it was just too early in the morning. The penetrating noise of the iron-wheeled alarm clock, or green goddesses as they were named, was the signal that persuaded my Dad to rouse himself from his sleep and commence his daily ritual. I would hear the springs of his bed complaining as he lifted his huge body to its feet, then listen to the creaking of his bedroom door as he eased it open. I saw the flicker of candlelight playing on my bedroom wall as Dad made his way in stockinged feet along the unlit landing and down the dark unlit stairway. I would lie in my bed and listen to the clanking of his enamelled slop bucket as it made frequent contact with the wooden bannisters. Once in the kitchen he would switch on the bare unshaded electric light bulb that hung from the centre of the ceiling. He would don his heavy hobnailed workman's boots, then make his way through to the back kitchen and into the back yard. His main target was the outside lavatory and I could hear his heavily studded boots performing a tattoo as they made contact with the cold hard slabs. We never had an inside toilet, nor a bathroom. Our only source of water was the lavatory and an inside cold tap over a brown earthenware sink in the back kitchen. If we wanted hot water we boiled it on the open fire. I would listen as Dad emptied his slops down the lavatory pan, then he would sit there awhile contemplating the day ahead — a sort of think-tank. When he had finished he would cleanse himself with a square of old damp newspaper from a batch that had been purposely prepared and nailed to the bare limewashed brick wall. The sound of coal being shovelled into the slop pail could now be heard. The coal was sometimes stored in the yard, at other times under the stairs, where it was accessible from the back kitchen. Sufficient kindle wood was chopped and old newspaper crunched to prepare the kitchen fire. Dad would first of all rake out the ashes left in the grate from the night before, then line it with the crunched paper and place the kindle wood above. On top of this he would gently place small pieces of coal. When the paper was lit he placed a shovel with a metal handle vertically above the fire bars to support a full sheet of old newspaper — the aim was to divert the air to below the fire bars where it would be fed to the paper, wood and coal and help to give maximum combustion to the fire. The paper would ignite and this would draw the air in beneath it. The kindle would then ignite and begin to crackle and the fire would roar. At this point the newspaper and shovel could be removed, before the newspaper caught alight, which it sometimes did, and sometimes the soot-encrusted chimney too. Dad would put more coal on the fire and top it off with the cinders from the previous night's fire, then collect the ashes and place them in the slop bucket.

From tens of thousands of chimneys, domestic, commercial and industrial, thick smoke would belch out to drift aloft into the heavenly atmosphere. The resultant smog was the soup that we were all accustomed to inhaling into our lungs. This made the urban populace of big cities prone to catarrhal symptoms and various other chest problems. What a wonderful, clean, clear and healthy environment we live in nowadays by comparison! But I must not digress.

Dad's domestic duties were once again complete for the morning. He would now prepare for work by donning his old, greasy gabardine, which had been waterproofed over the years by contact with industrial machinery. Gabardines were never washed — if a docker had had his mac washed he would have stood out like a sore thumb and have been ridiculed. Dad would place his equally greasy cap upon his head and stick his docker's hook firmly into his broad trouser belt. The final act was to wedge a pack of cheese or corned beef sandwiches, wrapped in old newspaper, into one pocket and a congealed mixture of tea, sugar and condensed milk, wrapped in greaseproof paper salvaged from American dried egg packets, into the other — the eggs were a product of America's Lend Lease policy. At seven precisely Dad would leave the house for work. The home was now a warm, cosy and safe refuge for Mother and her children to come down to. Having closed the door firmly behind him, Dad would walk almost a mile through the backstreets of Liverpool, his hobnailed boots beating out a steady rhythm as they made contact with the flagstones of the damp pavements. His destination was the 18A tramcar stop outside the Hippodrome Cinema. This would take him on a rattling ride through the Everton, Kirkdale, Bootle and Seaforth districts of Merseyside, culminating at the mouth of the River Mersey and Gladstone Dock, where, with others of his ilk, he would toil all day and sometimes all night, on many occasions seven days a week, loading and unloading merchant vessels from all corners of the world. During the Second World War he even worked while bombs dropped, loading ships with vital war material that was needed for fighting men battling against the enemy overseas, or for the Arctic convoys taking arms to help the Russians in their battle against the common, German, enemy. These ships had to be loaded in accord with a tight schedule in order to be ready to form up with other ships in Liverpool Bay. They would each have an allotted place in a moderately escorted merchant convoy. The convoy would cautiously move off, chaperoned by Royal Navy destroyers or frigates. When all was ready they would commence their dangerous voyage through open seas that were infested with merciless enemy submarines waiting at periscope depth, biding their time. The speed of the convoy was always governed by that of the slowest merchantman, who would be trailing in the rear.

What wonderful dreams Dad must have had over the years while he toiled at the docks, working on ships from across the world and mixing with all nationalities. And yet he never left the shores of his own country, Britain. Like millions of others, he simply could not afford to. The common working people only went abroad when their country required their services, to conquer new distant lands or defend ones already gained. It was hardy and stalwart men the likes of my Dad who helped to maintain the image of Great Britain in the eyes of foreigners. By comparison, the majority of today's men are no match for our forebears of yesteryear. They are overweight, over-indulgent, centrally heated, car-motivated, junk food-addicted and pathetic wimps whose main concern is the gratification of self.

CHAPTER
SIXTEEN

Salvage for the War Effort

Another preoccupation I shared with my siblings Monica and Gerald, and indeed many other kids, was collecting salvage for the war effort. Cardboard was the most prized possession, in pursuit of which we would go from shop to shop until the shopkeepers got sick of our pleadings. Whatever we had collected we took to school and put in a special storeroom the headmaster had put aside for cardboard and paper. All schools collected waste paper and there was great rivalry between the schools because when the waste was periodically collected it was weighed and the school with the highest amount was given a diploma. One day a call came over the wireless for old aluminium pots, pans and other items, which would be melted down and remade into aircraft parts. From the start of this campaign Monica, Gerald and I started to harangue Mother and the neighbours for their spare pots and pans. Mother didn't have any spare utensils and the ones she used daily had holes in them — they had been constantly repaired by Dad with pan menders that you bought from the chandlers. The pan repair kit consisted of two aluminium washers about 1 inch in diameter, each with a small hole in the centre, and with this was a cork washer of the same size and a small brass nut and bolt. To repair the pan you placed a washer on the inside then the cork with the other washer on the outside then bolted them all together.

In time, Monica, Gerald and I would expand our area of waste collection to the roads the other side of Kensington, because the people who lived there were more affluent. The houses were still terraced but had basements and were privately owned. Albany, Saxony, Albert Edward, Empress, Adelaide, Leopold, Edinburgh and Connaught Roads and Jubilee Drive — even the names were quite impressive. We borrowed the old pram, with Mother's consent but also a warning to keep an eye on it. The word aluminium was not a word than ran easily off our unaccustomed tongues. We would start our salvage campaign by splitting up and doing both sides of the road. Invariably a woman would open the front door in answer to my knocking. "What do you want, my love?" she would ask. I would stand there open mouthed.

"Errmmm" — my mind had gone blank and I would turn my back on the woman at the door and shout to my sister who was collecting on the other side of the road. "Ha! Mick! Micky! What's that stuff called?"

"Alimonion," she replied, but obviously the woman had heard the plea on her wireless. "Aluminium," she corrected. "Wait there a moment, son, I'll go and have a look in the scullery." We would continue our unpaid voluntary task for the war effort, knocking on many doors and collecting a good number of pots and pans. We only stopped collecting when Mother's washday pram was loaded to the gunnels. Then we would head home first to show Mam how successful we had been, before handing in our catch at the local police station as we had been instructed over the wireless.

When Mam saw our spoils she was amazed. Picking up a saucepan, she asked, "Who gave you these? They're much better than the ones I have."

"Then why don't you swap them, Mam?" Micky said.

"Oh, I daren't! Someone might see me," said Mother.

"I'll take the pram around the back entry, Mam, nobody will see you then," I said.

With the old pram safely in the back yard out of sight of peering eyes, Mother had a good rummage, selected a new set of second-hand pans, dumped her old patched pans into the pram and said, "Now go quickly and deliver these to the police station, Bryan, and don't say anything to anyone."

The desk sergeant was surprised when we walked into the Bridewell pushing our old pram loaded with scrap.

"What's all this then, giving yourselves up with your loot, are you?" he jokingly said.

"It's alimonion, sergeant, for making Spitfires and we've been collecting it," Micky explained.

"Right then, follow me with your wheelbarrow," he said.

"It's not a wheelbarrow, it's me Mam's pram and she wants it back," I told him.

We followed the sergeant down a long passageway until he stopped outside a cell. I had never been in a police station before, let alone a cell.

"Right now, unload your pram and stack it in there, then you can be free to collect some more."

"Sergeant, is this where you lock up murderers?" asked Micky.

"We certainly do, young lady, and if you come across any while you're collecting aluminium, you bring them back here to Sergeant Stripes."

We left the police station in a happy mood: we had a good collection and had seen the cells.

"Did you hear what that police sergeant called me?" said Micky.

"No, what was it?" asked Gerald.

"He called me a young lady. Nobody has ever called me that before."

There was a great demand for steel and iron among other raw materials for the war effort. Britain depended on the import of these commodities, but because of the huge amount of shipping that was being lost through enemy action, the government decreed that iron railings and such like that were not really necessary should be commandeered. The railings and ornamental iron gates for parks, cemeteries and other places were cut down by contractors using oxyacetylene cutters and taken away to smelting furnaces. If you look carefully today you can still see reminders of this activity in some areas, the little stubs of iron sticking out of low walls where the railings have been taken away.

CHAPTER
SEVENTEEN

Ernie Bradbury

In my spare time and in order to earn pocket money I would help Ernie Bradbury, who owned the shippin at the bottom of our street. I would spend many hours day in and day out with Ernie. He never really gave me a lot of money for the work I did, just the odd half a crown now and then, but sometimes five bob. I suppose he had about twenty cows, arranged two to a stall, all with names such as Daisy, Snowdrop, Daffodil and Tulip. They were always given the names of flowers but I don't know why. They were a mixed breed of cattle, black and white Friesians, brown and white Guernseys and brown Jerseys. Some had prize rosettes pinned to the wall above their heads. Ernie would sit on his three-legged milking stool, dressed in a brown cow gown, and with a galvanised bucket wedged firmly between his knees. I would mix cattle feed with water in big iron containers, then stir it to the consistency of porridge. These containers were quite heavy when they were full of cattle food. I would have to walk between the cows and put the container down under their snouts so they could feed. The cows were always tethered at the head but I would have to slap them on the rump to separate them, then force my way between them while struggling with the heavy container. I was never completely happy going between the cows, especially when they turned their heads towards me, mooed deeply or closed in on me — it always made me frightened. Another job I did was clearing out their straw bedding, which was saturated with urine and droppings. I would first rake the old bedding into the trough, which ran the full length of the shippin. Some overshot its target and some undershot it, depending on the position the animal was in when it decided to unload itself. I would then clear out the trough with a fork and load it into a wheelbarrow. If you can imagine the waste products of twenty cows over a twenty-four hour period, then you can also imagine how much clearing out I had to do. I would fill the wheelbarrow then laboriously push it outside the shippin to an external midden. Then I would fork it from the wheelbarrow into the midden over a 3ft brick wall. It was hard work for a young lad. After many trips with the wheelbarrow I would use a large spade to clear the final slops from the trough, bearing in mind that the cows were dropping faeces and urinating all the time.

When the cows had finished eating I would fill their containers with water by the bucketful. Cows drink a lot of water — they have to otherwise they would produce dried milk, and customers are none too keen on dried milk. At the least three buckets of water in each container and there were twenty containers, which makes sixty buckets. I know this and I'm innumerate. By using two buckets I cut down the watering trips to thirty. Meanwhile, Ernie would go from cow to cow fondling their udders and manipulating their teats in a rhythmic fashion, thereby relieving them of their precious milk. The milk squirted into his galvanised pail, making a most harmonious sound in the process. Ernie loved his cattle. The shippin was his personal harem and he knew how to get the best from each one of his female beasts. Between tasks I would stand and watch Ernie perform his cowshed symphony. There were always a couple of cats hanging around in the yard and they would knowingly make their way to the shippin when it was milking time and stand expectantly close to the cow that Ernie was milking. Ernie would aim the cow's teat at the cats and fire a stream of warm milk that would hit the cats in the faces. Instead of moving away they sat there licking the milk from their fur.

"What do you want doing now, Ernie?" I would enquire. Ernie kept to his perfect rhythm, the cap on his head snuggling into the cow's side as he worked. He'd have a cigarette stuck in the corner of his mouth, his head cocked to one side, and blow the ash from his cigarette and talk to me from the other side of his mouth.

"Pass me the cats' dish and I'll give them some milk, Bryan, then go into the loft and drop some cattle cake and a handful of hay down the hatches, then drop some fresh straw down and put it underneath the cows, that's a good lad."

"OK, Ernie!" I'd respond. This was a job I liked doing. I would climb the vertical wooden ladder that was fixed to the shippin wall and go into the loft. Next I would open the wooden hatch door to the stall that Ernie was milking in, break up a slab of cattle cake and drop it to the cows, then follow it with a good armful of hay. Then I would poke my head out of the hatch and say, "How's that, Ernie?"

"That's ample, Bryan. If we give them too much they'll have indigestion and end up with horrible nightmares." I would continue down the line of hatches dropping cattle cake and hay to the animals below, and when that was done I would drop down their bedding. If the cows had moved to the middle of the stall the straw would end up on their heads and hang off their horns like Easter bonnets. Coming down again from the loft I would make the cows comfortable for the night by spreading straw between them to lie upon. The next job was to sweep the general area clean and spread sawdust into the trough and onto the cobbled walkway.

When Ernie's milk bucket was full he would take it into the dairy next door and empty the contents into a milk cooler, from which the milk would trickle down through a succession of horizontal bars into a milk churn. Ernie then returned to the shippin and continued his milking. A man working on a part-time basis in the evenings did various tasks within the dairy. Ernie did not have many milk bottles or crates, and so these were kept clean and sterilised by his assistant, who would then fill them with milk by hand and place a cardboard stopper in the lip of each bottle, swill the whole crate down with cold water and place it in the cold room until the morning. The bulk of the milk would be left in churns and also placed into the cold room, any surplus milk being turned into cream, butter and cheese. A simple hand-turned centrifuge machine was used to separate the milk into skimmed milk or curds and whey.

The butter, cheese and eggs produced were sold in Mrs Bradbury's shop, but only to private and privileged customers who could afford the price Mrs Bradbury demanded for her fresh and unrationed merchandise. There was never an official ration of eggs, but when they were in the grocer's they were issued as perhaps one egg per ration book, or just one egg on a baby's green ration book. It was rumoured that Mrs Bradbury was into the black market and bartered her dairy produce for other commodities such as sugar, coffee and tea. Ernie's mother was an old widow. She would come through into the shippin from her house and shop carrying a tray with tea and egg sandwiches made from white home-made bread. This was mainly for her son, but Ernie's assistant and I were never left out. Mrs Bradbury was on a food ration like the rest of us, but she always made her own bread, which was beautiful and white, and because Ernie ran the dairy she had plenty of cream, butter, cheese and eggs. On occasion Ernie would tell me to search the loft for eggs. He kept free-range hens up there, who laid eggs wherever they could — you had to be careful you did not stand on them. There were also rabbits running wild up there, and no doubt rats too. I would collect the eggs in a wicker basket and take them into Mrs Bradbury's shop. Ernie also had a couple of pigs in his yard, which lived mostly on scrap food — fortunately pigs will eat anything that is edible and miraculously transform it into delicious bacon and other human delicacies. A pig wastes nothing and nothing from a pig is wasted.

Sometimes when Ernie and I were working, the air-raid sirens would sound and Ernie would say, "Make sure them fire buckets are full, Bryan, then you had better get off home. Your mother will be getting worried about you." But I might linger on a bit until I heard the anti-aircraft guns open up. Ernie would continue milking his cows, undaunted by the potential danger and never seeking shelter. He was a fatalist: "If your name's on it, then it'll get you," he would say. Incendiary bombs were Ernie's main worry, with all the inflammable material in the loft and of course the shippin itself, which was mainly of timber construction.

"Do you want me in the morning, Ernie?" I would ask before leaving.

"Yes, Bryan, but be as early as possible." When I left the cows would be mooing apprehensively as the guns fired and Ernie would talk quietly to them as he continued to milk. "Never you mind, Daisy, that's only a bit of thunder," he would say. Ernie worked extremely long hours. He was one of the hardest workers that I have ever come across.

My father, Ernie Bradbury and one or two other men were role models for me: I have nothing but praise for each and every one of them. I like to think that some of their tenacity, loyalty and industry has rubbed off on me and helped me to struggle my way through the pitfalls of life. Ernie not only had the cows to look after, there were the pigs, the hens, the cats, the rabbits, his horse, and of course his ageing mother. He was married and had children and lived on the other side of Kensington in Albert Edward Road. When the raids were on he must have been very concerned about them, but despite his divided loyalties he was like a soldier on duty and had to stick to his post.

"Where have you been, Bryan? In that shippin again to this hour — don't you realise there's a raid on?"

"Sorry, Mam! I came home straight away."

"Straight away! The raid's been on half an hour, can't you hear the guns? I shouldn't have to go looking for you, I can't just leave the young ones on their own."

"Where's me Dad, Mam?"

"He's not home from work yet. Look at the state of you! You're filthy and stink of cow muck. Go and wash yourself and change your clothes, then eat your dinner. It's been in the oven all night and'll be dried up now and stuck to the plate, and don't touch your father's, yours is on the bottom shelf."

"Oh thanks, Mam! I like it like that when I've got to chisel it off with a knife. The crusty bits are nice."

"Then make sure you wash your plate after you and put it away on the Welsh dresser."

"Can I go with Ernie tomorrow, Mam?"

"Has he asked you?"

"Yiss, he told me to be early."

"All right then! But don't be too late home, do you understand, Bryan?"

Air raids occurred over a period of three years from 5 June 1940 until 10 January 1942. I was therefore over eight years of age at the beginning of the raids and over ten at the end. They occurred intermittently throughout this period except during the May blitz of 1941 when Merseyside was bombed for eight consecutive nights with a total of 800 German Dornier bombers dropping their loads of high-explosive bombs, incendiary bombs and land mines. On reflection, I was about ten years old when I first started to help Ernie Bradbury, and this was mostly in the summer holiday periods.

Ernie had very little sleep at night, but I think he would cat nap during the daytime if he had a chance. I got to the shippin at about eight-thirty the following morning, and Ernie was already there. He was just taking his horse from the stable and putting it into the middle of the yard where the milk float was parked with its shafts pointing towards the sky.

"Good morning, Bryan! Now, can you just hold the horse's reins while I lower the shafts?"

"OK, Ernie."

Ernie had already dressed the horse in its shining leather harness; now it was a matter of hooking the harness up to the shafts. At this point the horse was eating its morning provender from a nosebag, which kept it from being irritable while Ernie was working with it. The milk float had two iron-rimmed wheels about 4ft 6in in diameter, each with shaped wooden mudguards, varnished and decorated. The sides and front of the float were built up, and half of the back was built up too. You got onto the float by stepping onto a little iron step fixed to the back and pulled yourself up by a couple of hand rails, then stepped through a gap and onto the platform. The gap had a little hinged door for safety. The float was a beautiful object, and was made of various types of varnished and highly polished hardwood. The chassis was made of iron and steel and the suspension of leaf springs set in a happy-mouthed arch. The shafts were fixed rigidly to the chassis and were very slender and beautifully contoured. The fittings on the shafts and the float were made of highly polished brass. To ride in Ernie's milk float was a dream and I absolutely loved it.

The next job was for Ernie to take two full milk churns and four crates of milk from the cold room, and lift them onto the back of the float. I couldn't help him with these, as they were too heavy for me to lift. I would stand on the floor of the float and try to assist him as he landed them. The churns and crates were kept at the front of the float and Ernie and I stayed at the back. In this way the float was nicely balanced, with the shafts tending neither to lift the horse nor exert too much pressure. The nosebag was taken off the horse and hung at the front of the float, then I would hold up a bucket of water for the horse to drink and Ernie would place the horse's bit into its mouth. Finally he would sling his brown leather cash bag over his shoulder and we would be ready for off. Holding the reins, Ernie would steer the horse and float out of the yard and up Fielding Street. We would then cut across Kensington to the well-to-do houses on the other side. The horse would run at a gentle trot, the sound of its hooves beating a retreat on the metalled surface of the road, the iron-framed wheels making a pleasant sound as they too made contact with the road's surface. Ernie would sit on a little collapsible seat connected to the rear of the float, while I would stand next to him with a firm grip on the brass hand rail. When Ernie came to a junction he would always stand up and move as far forward as he could, crane his neck, slow the horse down to a walk, then negotiate the junction. He had regular customers and most of the time he knew exactly what they wanted.

"Two bottles for No. 8 and one for No. 10, Bryan." I would jump from the float and place the order onto the steps and pick up the empty bottles.

"Watch that you don't stand on my steps, young man!" This instruction came from a large lady who was on her knees scrubbing the two steps that led up to her front door, a custom that you do not see today. If we were delivering to a series of houses, then Ernie would lead the horse from the front. Sometimes he got well in front, and when this happened he would call to the horse, who would gently walk towards him. The side roads were always quiet and devoid of traffic. Nobody had cars so it was easy for the horse and he never bumped into anything. The other regular traffic was the coal man's horse and cart or the man selling huge blocks of salt, or the man selling vegetables, or perhaps a hand cart.

"Pick up those jugs, Bryan, at No. 22 and 24!" People would leave containers on their steps, ready to be filled, often with saucers on top to stop the cats thieving the milk. Ernie had a long-handled metal scoop hanging inside a churn. It was a pint measure, and with it he would put the appropriate amount of milk in the jugs, sometimes one pint, sometimes two, sometimes a half. If it was half a pint he would still use the same scoop, fill up the container, pour some back into the churn then pour the rest into the jug.

"How do you know that was half a pint, Ernie?" I once asked him.

"It's quite simple, Bryan," he said. "You fill the scoop which is one pint then pour some of it back into the churn until you can just see the bottom of the scoop appear, then that is half a pint." I was amazed. It's so simple, provided that the scoop is cylindrical, and it's something that I have never forgotten. Everybody liked Ernie and they liked his horse too. Old ladies would save up their old crusts of bread to feed it, and stand at the horse's head with bread in their hands, stroking and feeding it.

"Come along now, Mrs Hopkins, that's enough. You'll have him as big as an elephant, then I won't be able to get him between the shafts." Halfway through the day Ernie would stop at his own home, refill the nosebag and fasten it to the horse's snout. "Come on in, Bryan, let's go and have a cup of tea. Bring three bottles with you, and I'll carry the eggs."

Mrs Bradbury was pleasant enough. She always treated me right, except that I had the feeling she was talking about me to Ernie. It was not an open conversation because her words were guarded so that I was not quite aware of what was going on, but I sensed she was criticising me in some obscure way. Perhaps it was the way I looked — scrawny, hungry-looking, shabbily dressed. I suppose I was over-sensitive, but I could detect this silent criticism, and it's not a nice thing to experience. Apart from that she was kind to me and would offer me food and drink. Ernie had a couple of children but I did not take too much notice of them except for the fact that they were younger than me, well mannered, well fed and well dressed. I think one was a boy and the other a girl.

There were lots of privately run dairies in Liverpool. Ernie's brother Edgar had one in the West Derby area and I would help him on occasions. He didn't have a horse and float but a small van, and sometimes in the summer he would have his cattle delivered to a field by cattle truck for grazing. They would stay in the open field for months, and we would go there with cattle food for them. When we got there they were always at the top end of the field.

"Go and chase them down, Bryan," Edgar would tell me. It was a daunting task to have to go into that field of cows then get around the back of them and "shoo" them towards Edgar. Meanwhile, Edgar would be getting cattle food from the back of the van together with his milking stool, bucket and churn. With a lot of hand clapping, shouting and waving from me together with Edgar proffering cow cake, the cows would eventually make their way to the rendezvous point.

I was in Ernie's shippin one night performing my usual tasks when the door opened and a huge lad entered. He was the son of another dairy man, who had a place in Boaler Street. He had been sent down to Ernie's place by his father on an errand. It must have been late August or early September because the lad was eating plums from a brown paper bag, and they could not have been imported. As he stepped onto the wet floor of the shippin he lost his footing and ended up on his backside. His beautiful black plums shot from his hand, rolled across the floor and ended up in the trough. He was none too pleased about losing his plums or about the state his trousers were in.

"Oh dear!" remarked Ernie. "Are you all right, Simon?"

The lad answered in the affirmative, conveyed his message to Ernie, then left the shippin. I pondered for a brief moment in the course of my duties. It would be a shame to shovel the plums up and throw them in the midden with the rest of the cow droppings, I thought, so I didn't, but gently picked up the fruits one by one and placed them in a bucket and ran the cold tap over them. To this day I insist that those plums were the tastiest I have ever eaten.

It was still daylight and the calm of the evening was broken by the sound of fast-moving aeroplanes, then the rattle of rapid gun fire; yet the sirens had not sounded.

"See you tomorrow, Ernie!" I shouted, and fled the shippin. I raced up Fielding Street like a March hare. People were out on the pavements looking up into the clear blue sky. I could see Mother and Father, and slowly realised what they were looking at: it was a dog fight between Spitfires and Messerschmitt 109s. I ran behind Mam and Dad and into the house — they never even saw me, I was that fleet of foot. Then I heard them shouting towards the end of the street. "Bryan, Bryan, where are you?"

"I'm here, Mam!" I replied.

Mother and Father then went into the house, and shouted from the kitchen, "Where are you?"

"I'm here, Mam, under the stairs!" The evidence of that dog fight could be seen in the form of bullet holes in the sandstone lintel of the house next door to ours, No. 18, until it was demolished alongside ours, No. 20, many years later during slum clearance.

CHAPTER
EIGHTEEN

The USA Enters the War

On 7 December 1941 the imperial Japanese nation attacked the American naval base at Pearl Harbor without any warning whatsoever. The destruction and carnage was terrible, but this action was to prove the most disastrous move that Japan could have made. They had now touched the raw nerve of the world's greatest industrialised free nation. On the following day, 8 December 1941, the USA declared war on Japan, meaning that the Allies were now led by the USA in their battle against the Axis powers. Britain had been hoping for some time that the USA would enter the war in the West against Germany, and now it had. This was the beginning of the end for Japan and Germany and those who supported them, and American industry was now mobilised as never before. In 1942 American airmen and war planes began to arrive in Britain and not long after American troopships and transports would be tying up at the Pier Head landing stage on the River Mersey.

The river and its approaches were protected by anti-aircraft balloons and ack-ack batteries. These balloons were mostly anchored to small river boats and were smaller than those used on land. Their aim was to deter dive-bombers. I would regularly walk to the Pier Head and watch the ever-changing scene. There would be armed sentries on the dock gates to Prince's Landing Stage so I could not get as close as I would have liked. Monica and I would spend a lot of time mooching about the Pier Head as there was always something to see and the river was always busy with ships ploughing up and down its length — steamers, tankers, dredgers, tug boats, ships of all shapes and sizes, some showing the scars of war and the rusting effects of age. There were also naval ships, corvettes and destroyers, with their distinctive grey-blue colour. The destroyers also gave an unmistakable blast from their steam whistles, a high-pitched "whoop whoop whoop".

The entrances and ground-floor windows of important buildings such as Royal Liver, Cunard, Mersey Docks and Harbour Board were protected by walls of sandbags. Micky had a thing about sailors in uniform and would touch their collars for luck. She especially liked the Free French sailors because they wore a red pompom on their hats.

I would stand on the corner of Fielding Street and Kensington for hours at a time watching the military convoys making their way inland to a transit camp in the Liverpool suburb of Huyton. Monica and I would cheer the truckloads of incoming American troops as they passed by. The city centre at this time became thronged with servicemen and women in uniform, mostly Yanks of course but there were also Canadians and other Commonwealth troops, including the remnants of defeated European nations — these were known as the Free French, Free Dutch, Free Poles and so on. The Yanks were well dressed and had plenty of money, so they were an immediate target for the Liverpool judies. Monica and I would walk to town with our autograph books and ask men in uniform for their signatures. Once we had acquired an autograph we would then go on the scrounge. "Got any gum, chum?" I would ask as an opening gambit, and Micky would follow with, "Got any chocolate, Charlie?" The Yanks were quite generous to us scrawny kids and seldom refused, saying, "Here you are, young Limey, now run off home to your Ma."

When we did go home we would tell Mam of our exploits and show her the money that we had scrounged, English, American, Canadian, French, Dutch, in fact money from most of the foreign nationals who had fled to Britain from Nazi-occupied Europe. And we would also show her our autograph books. She would glance through them and make comments like, "Oh that's nice!" and "I like that one, but don't tell your father that you have been down town, and don't show him that foreign money."

The war began to turn in favour of the Allies, shipping losses were being drastically curtailed and the German Panzer divisions were being pushed back across eastern Europe by the Russian advances. The bombing of Germany was stepped up as the RAF bombed by night and the AAF by day. There were air raids on Germany in the order of a thousand bombers at a time, which must have taken a great deal of planning. The planes on these missions would fly from all over Britain and when this happened everybody knew about it because you could not sleep at night for the constant drone of Allied bombers flying high above and eastwards.

The Yanks were very popular with the women and, of course, there were plenty of women — and not all single. Some women whose husbands were away on active service took advantage of this fresh importation of virile young men. Criticism of the Yanks came from many quarters, and they were often referred to as "over-sexed, over-paid and over here". The Grafton Dance Hall in West Derby Road was a favourite venue for the Yanks on a Saturday night, and also for the Liverpool judies. Although the Yanks were a mixture of blacks and whites, racism was rampant — the Americans had brought it over with them. And racism would manifest itself in the Grafton on a Saturday night when fighting broke out between rival factions. American Military Police would be called in to quell the trouble, and they would remain on duty both inside and outside the dance hall with military trucks waiting outside to take the offenders back to camp and the detention block. The GIs brought jiving and jitterbugging to the dance halls of Britain, along with Lucky Strike cigarettes, Yankee comics and nylons. You could not condemn the girls for falling prey to this sort of bait in an impoverished and heavily rationed Britain. And of course when man meets woman sparks fly and the result is babies, in this case war babies. Unfortunately, these American GIs and Canadians together with British and Polish troops were part of the huge military build-up for the opening of the second front. On 6 June 1944 this front opened with the invasion of Normandy, and many of those war babies would never see their fathers.

There was a certain lady in Fielding Street whose husband was away serving with the RAF. Blondie, as she was called, was well known to entertain the GIs. She was one of the posh ones in our street. Her husband used to work as the local representative of an insurance company before the war. The company had a highly polished brass plate fitted to the wall of his house beside the front door to tell the world that he was an insurance agent. They had no children so when her husband was away fighting for his country his wife was doing her social bit by entertaining his Allies. As inquisitive kids we would see her guests entering the house rather furtively by way of the back door. By listening to neighbours jangling we soon learned the reason for these surreptitious and nocturnal visits.

It goes without saying that during the war there was full employment, as there was a great demand for labour. Women worked on the land, forming the Land Army, and also in munitions factories and on the tram cars. Ireland was a neutral country but the Irish flocked to Britain in hundreds of thousands seeking to fill the void in the labour market created by British manpower fighting the enemy. In our street a certain Mrs Ford and her husband Arthur, who lived at No. 6, used the spare rooms of their three-storey house to take in Irish lodgers. Mrs Ford used to come to our house regularly to gossip with Mother, and of course I would be there to listen in.

One day she was telling Mother about her new lodgers. They were hard-working, as most Irish men are, and after a hard day's labour they would retire to the local public house for liquid refreshments before going back to their lodgings for dinner. Public houses closed at ten o'clock in those days. As Mrs Ford's house conformed to the norm in having no inside toilet, she issued her lodgers with an enamel slop bucket to take up to bed with them because, being a worldly woman, she realised that their intake of liquid would pressurise their bladders during the night and trying to negotiate two flights of steps during the blackout period could end in disaster. In the mornings Mrs Ford, along with her general duties of making the beds and tidying up the bedrooms, would collect the slop pail and empty it in the outside lavatory. But one morning it was raining rather heavily and in order to keep herself dry she placed the brimming slop pail temporarily in the back kitchen while she went about performing her other household duties. It was a Friday, and although she was a non-practising Protestant herself she was aware of the religious duties of the Roman Catholic Irish. Not wanting to displease her lodgers she diligently headed for town and made haste for St John's fish market. Returning happily with her purchase, Mrs Ford settled down to preparing the evening meal of finnan haddock, mashed potatoes and peas. Unfortunately, she forgot that she had not emptied the pail of urine, and while unloading her shopping bag the haddock was knocked accidentally into the stale liquid. Mrs Ford faced a dilemma: food was hard to come by, and so was money for that matter, and the market would soon be closed and was a long way off. Her primary concern was for her loyal, hard-working Irish lodgers. There was only one thing to do: to retrieve the fish from the bucket of urine, wash it thoroughly under a tap of cold running water, cook it then serve it up — after all, she thought, it was their own urine.

With a certain amount of trepidation, Mrs Ford watched her lodgers eat their evening meal after they had returned from the local pub.

"Well, boys, how was your dinner?" she enquired.

"Oh now, Mrs Ford, that was indeed a lovely bit of fish," remarked Patrick.

"Oh God, Mrs Ford, you're such a wonderful cook!" observed Michael.

"Well, boys, I'm really glad that you enjoyed it," she countered. "I do like to see hard-working men enjoying their evening meal. I'll bid you good night now and I'll see you in the morning. By the way, you'll find your pail in your bedroom."

The Ford family got on extremely well with their lodgers, to the extent that one of the lodgers returned from a Christmas visit to his mother in Ireland and brought back a large oven-ready goose for his landlady by way of a Christmas present. Mrs Ford was eternally grateful for this unrationed meat and her gratitude knew no bounds.

"I'll roast it in the oven and we'll have it on Sunday, together with roast potatoes and all the trimmings. It'll be just like another Christmas dinner," she said.

Sunday came and the goose went into the oven, but about two hours later there was an almighty explosion in the kitchen: the oven door had blown off, the contents were scattered around the room and anything that could ignite was ablaze. Fortunately Mrs Ford was not in the kitchen at the time, but she was close at hand, jangling with neighbours on her front door step. The blaze was immediately tackled by local members of the ARP with their stirrup pumps, used for such emergencies. The fire brigade was also quickly on the scene and stopped the fire from spreading. Mrs Ford's kitchen, however, was gutted. An inquiry was set up to ascertain the cause of the explosion, although it was presumed that Mrs Ford had turned on the gas but forgotten to ignite it. Mrs Ford herself was more concerned with the loss of her goose than she was with the loss of her kitchen. "How will I explain it to the boys when they come home from work? It was such a lovely big goose, and what will I give them now for dinner?" Later that evening, when most of the mess was cleaned up and the kitchen made semi-functional once again, the hungry lodgers returned from their labours via the local watering hole. They worked ten-hour shifts for seven days a week on various government-ordained projects, such as army barracks, airfields and ammunition factories.

"Oh now, begorra! What's happened here, Mrs Ford? Has there been an air raid while we have been away?"

"No, Patrick, there hasn't. The oven just exploded and the goose was blown to smithereens," said Mrs Ford.

"Well now, bejazus, how could that happen?" enquired Patrick.

"I think that I forgot to light the gas," explained Mrs Ford.

"Did you happen to find me bottle of whiskey at all?" quizzed Michael.

"Wherever did you leave it, Michael?" asked Mrs Ford.

Michael looked at Mrs Ford with mouth agape and replied rather sheepishly, "I left it inside the goose, Mrs Ford, and I forgot to take it out."

CHAPTER
NINETEEN

Victory

D-Day, 6 June 1944, was a day that I shall never forget. This was the day when the Allies invaded Normandy, a day that changed the course of the war. I was now twelve years of age and for me this was exhilarating news. Dad was the first in our street to feel that victory was not far off. I remember reading the headlines in the *Liverpool Echo* on the evening of that historic day: "Allies invade northern France . . . 10,000 ships and thousands of other craft . . . everything going according to plan and what a plan." It's very hard to explain the amazing, spiritual uplifting that this wonderful news gave to the people of war-ravaged Britain.

"Get a bucket of limewash made up, Bryan, and write the word VICTORY on all of those air-raid shelters in big letters 6ft high."

"OK, Dad, I'll start right away." I really enjoyed myself doing this, and the neighbours cheered me on. When I was finished I was covered in lime from head to toe and was brought rudely to my senses by Mother, who had been shopping and spotted me on her way back.

"Bryan, what do you think you are doing? Look at your clothes!"

"It's OK, Mam, I'm doing a job for Dad."

"Did he tell you to paint yourself as well? Get into the house and change your clothes."

Dad was a great advocate for the opening of the second front. He wanted the pressure to be taken off our allies the Soviet Union, as did many other Socialists with communist sympathies. He had witnessed the birth of the Soviet Union in 1917 when the hungry workers of Russia revolted against the Tsar and formed the Red Army, installing the first communist democracy in the world. Now the Nazis' Panzer divisions were trying their utmost to crush the Red Army and conquer the fledgling workers' state. Communism became a dirty word in later years through the pressures of the capitalist West and its control of the media. The West did not want a workers' state to be successful because it knew it would mean the end of capitalism and the evil that went with it. But we must never forget that in this war at least Russia was our ally and fighting the same fight, a fight against tyranny and evil. The Liverpool dockers were a hard-working, unified and militant body of men who knew the score, who lived and worked close to the pulse of the war and loaded ships with arms and material for the Russian Front. These Russian convoys would brave Arctic waters infested with German U-boats in order to deliver their cargoes. In these years the photographs of Churchill, Eisenhower and Stalin standing side by side were seen regularly in the press and on posters. Dad had a large picture of Joseph Stalin — or Uncle Joe, as Dad called him — on display in the front window and another in the kitchen. Dad even commissioned Mother to make a flag for him. She dyed an old bed sheet brilliant red then cut out the hammer and sickle from some yellow material and sewed it on. The flag was about 8ft square and Dad connected it to the top of his wireless aerial and flew it proudly in the Mersey breeze for all to see.

At last the news coming out of the wireless was 90 per cent good. The Allies were still sustaining losses in men and material but they were liberating vast areas of land and freeing millions of oppressed people from slavery. The Nazis' last-ditch effort was to destroy London with their V1s and V2s, the flying bombs and doodlebugs, which thankfully could not reach Liverpool. The end of the war was now coming to a rapid conclusion, with the Red Army advancing into Germany from the east, the Western Allies advancing from the west and from the south through Italy. When the Germans finally capitulated on 8 May 1945, VE day was announced (Victory in Europe).

Euphoria broke out all over the Western world. People celebrated in pubs and danced in the streets, and ships blew their foghorns on the River Mersey. I remember the street lights being switched on again after being checked out, bonfires being lit in the streets and church bells ringing again. It was marvellous. The blackout was now over and we had a huge fire in the centre of Fielding Street, between the Royal Arch pub and Scott's the grocer's. We kids constantly fed the flames with anything that would burn, including doors and floorboards from derelict buildings. All the mothers and fathers and adults were milling around happily watching the flames and constantly popping in and out of the local for a beer. Everybody was happy, people were singing and we kids were no exception.

"I wonder where the little buggers are getting all this wood from?" said Mrs Jones.

"They're collecting it from the old bombed garage in Kensington," replied Mrs Ford.

Then suddenly Mother shouted: "Bryan! You can't burn that, that's my back door." She had spotted the big number twenty painted on the back of it.

"Don't worry, Mam, we will be getting a new house now that the war is over!" I said to her. In my simple mind I thought that the end of the war would mean the end of rationing, the end of slum conditions and a brand new world opening up for us all, with peace and prosperity for everyone. But of course things don't happen quite like that. In fact we were soon to have more rationing — even bread, which had never been rationed during the war, was now to be rationed. We had beaten the Germans, but the Japanese were not finished yet, and somebody had to pay for this costly war: the only people who can pay are the people who produce the goods and pay the taxes. My youthful dream of a brand new and peaceful world with food in abundance and happiness for all was but an idealist's dream.

The Japanese capitulation came four months later, on 2 September 1945 — my birthday. I was now fourteen years of age. This was the beginning of the atomic age, when the dropping of atomic bombs on the Japanese cities of Hiroshima and Nagasaki had finally brought the imperialistic Japanese to their senses.

VJ day was celebrated in grand style just like VE day, but now the streets were decked out with home-made bunting and placards, and there was talk of demobilisation of the armed forces and the repatriation of prisoners of war from the Far East. There were many street parties, especially when POWs were expected to be returning to their homes. Huge signs across streets proclaimed "Welcome Home Johnny, Japanese POW for three years!" or "Welcome Home Bill after four years in Burma!" Coupled with the happiness was sadness too, because a lot of Johnnys and a lot of Bills would never return to their homes. The world would be left with millions of weeping mothers, lonely widows and orphaned children. This is the ridiculous and incalculable price that we all must pay for mindless, bloody conflict.

When the war was over the authorities decided that certain kids needed a break from wartime routine. I was selected among others to have two weeks in Wales as a sort of convalescence for blitz kids. I was taken to the Ribble bus station in town by Mother, with a bag of clean clothes and a brown cardboard label pinned to my jacket lapel, with my details on it. I sat on the single-decker Ribble coach and waved goodbye to my mother. I was most excited about the trip but as I looked at my mother's sad face on parting I had to stifle a feeling of woe. The coach trip was exciting for us lads. We passed military encampments as we travelled through Cheshire and into Wales, and I remember seeing hundreds of khaki tents in neat regimented rows. Then the coach dropped us off at a camp site just outside the very small town of Mold in North Wales. We were shepherded into wooden buildings and allocated a wooden bunk each, in small rooms that afforded two two-tier bunks. All the kids were lads and the people who looked after us were all men. The days were well organised, with rambles in the woods, hill climbing, playing football and indoor games when it rained.

The mess hall was warm and cosy and the smell of food was inviting. We never entered the mess hall until the large external handbell was rung vigorously, then we would seat ourselves on long wooden forms each side of a wooden table. When the food was cooked and ready for serving the two end boys from each table nearest the servery would collect two dinners and put them down in front of the second two boys, and would then return for two more meals. Meanwhile, the two lads who had received the dinners would pass them to the next two, until they reached the lads at end of the table. Nobody was allowed to touch the food until everybody had been served, including the permanent staff, then we would all say grace. It seemed a very long wait when you were hungry and the food was tickling your nostrils. When dinner was over, all the plates would be moved along to the servery end of the table and the same two boys would pick up the plates and carry them to the dirty-dish counter. The boys would then collect the desserts and issue them in the same fashion, and when everyone had been served then we could eat. After this we again said grace, and the permanent staff instructed us on our seating arrangements from then onwards. The two boys who had served the meals today would sit at the far end of the table tomorrow and everybody would move towards the servery by one place. When you think about it, this was an efficient and simple method, with the minimum number of people on their feet, thereby reducing the number of possible accidental collisions and the mess they could incur, and it also took the pressure off the servery staff.

I enjoyed the countryside. It was a very hilly area with deep dark woods to play in. Everything was organised and I liked it that way. We would be about a mile away from camp and could just see it across a deep valley when we would hear the bell ringing out for the evening meal — it was a lovely welcoming sound. Then after a week had gone by I was befriended by a boy who was homesick, who asked if I would help him to find his way home. Without thinking of the consequences I said yes. I was quite happy with the camp myself and didn't want to leave, but the boy kept pestering me. I was young and impressionable and so one evening, just before dinner time, we headed for the nearest road, just a country lane, and we started to walk along it. I had no idea where I was heading for. We hadn't gone very far when one of the permanent staff caught up with us in his little van, questioned both of us then took us back to camp where we were interrogated further. The next day we were driven back home. This was a very disappointing period in my

126

young life; but I think and hope that I have learned from that experience, not to be coerced into things that I really don't want to do by others who lack the will to act on their own.

CHAPTER
TWENTY

The Boxing Club

The Kensington Gym, which stood over Scott's the grocer's, was owned by Les Douglas, a former lightweight professional boxer whose head bore all the standard hallmarks of a veteran pugilist, a twisted and broken nose, cauliflower ears and scarred eyebrows. He was a dapper little man, quick-witted, agile, fit and always smartly dressed. Two of his brothers, Sid and Rodney, had also been professional scrappers. The gym comprised a weight-training area on the ground floor, with a boxing ring on the first floor taking up one room, with another room for skipping. On the second floor was a room with punchbags and punchballs, a changing room and shower, and Les's small office. The whole place was a bit worse for wear, smelling terribly of mildew, damp and cold body sweat, but it served the basic purpose. A number of well-known professional boxers and wrestlers either trained or had trained there on a regular basis, the likes of Billy Wattleworth, Joe Curran, Nel Tarlton, Ernie Roderick, to name but a few. There was also a thriving amateur boxing team and others who went just to keep fit generally; and of course in those days no women participated.

It was Dad who first introduced me to the boxing club. One day he said to me, "Bryan, I want you to learn the noble art of self-defence and the Queensberry rules."

"What's all that about, Dad?" I asked.

"The laws of boxing," Dad replied.

"You shouldn't make him do that," said Mother. "He'll end up looking like Les Douglas and his lot, all battered and cut and with a broken nose."

"It's what he needs," said Dad to Mother. "You don't want him growing up like a wet nellie do you?"

"No, I don't want him growing up into a wet nellie, but I don't want him growing up as a punch drunk either," Mother retorted.

"Don't you worry, son, you won't be in any danger. I'll see to that, and it'll make a man out of you. You've got to learn how to defend yourself. There are a lot of evil scallywags out there always looking for trouble, and I want you to be able to look after yourself."

Mother reluctantly fell in line with Dad's plans, then set herself to work and made me a pair of boxing shorts in the colour of the Kensington boxing team, which was green. She also sewed my initials on the left leg in big letters: JBK.

"It's only two bob a week," said Dad, "and I'll pay that. You will be able to go there anytime that you want to, and after you have trained you will be able to have a hot shower, so remember to take a towel and soap with you."

"Yes, and remember to bring them back again!" said Mother.

Any lingering doubts I had about boxing were dispelled by the thought of a hot shower. That was luxury beyond belief — I had never had a hot shower in my life; in fact I had never experienced a cold shower. Nobody I knew had a bathroom, never mind a shower; in fact nobody I knew had running hot water.

There was a well-organised group of young boxers at the club, but I was probably one of the youngest. To begin with I was initiated into the techniques of skipping, which is a boxer's main form of physical exercise as it promotes stamina, expands the lungs and makes you light on your feet. Then there was the art of shadow boxing, which might seem silly to the uninitiated but is essential for gaining speed in moving around the ring and changing your stance while throwing punches and parrying punches with an imaginary opponent.

When Les spotted you shadow boxing he always had something to say. "Don't let him get you into a corner . . . turn the tables on him . . . watch his left jab . . . go for him now one two one two." To Les it wasn't just an imaginary opponent, it was real flesh and blood that you were up against. Then there were the punchbag and punchball to develop your punching ability and increase your speed, and of course a small amount of weight training to improve your physique and thereby improve your strength. The final training was actual boxing with other opponents in the ring. We novices and amateurs would study the professionals going through their paces encouraged by their managers. We were keen to pick up technical tips from them, so we watched them keenly whenever they were at the club training for their next fight, and it was specially good to see them in the ring. Sometimes you could not get near them for all the media reporters and photographers. The room the ring was in was not very big and the free space would be packed to capacity.

"More Tiger! More Tiger!" This was Les's encouragement to us youngsters whenever he entered the room while we were using the punchbags. He would come up to you when you were punching the bag, tear into it himself with solid punches but without making the bag sway.

"Now that's the way to do it Bryan. Solid punching straight from the shoulder and bags of tiger, bags of tiger." We bandaged our hands for protection when using the bags, otherwise the skin would have come off with all the constant punching. Les said, "In the bare-knuckle days of yesteryear boxers soaked their hands in their own urine to harden them before a fight."

"Oh, I don't think me mam would like that!" I told him.

Another technique for stamina was what was known as road work. We would be out on the roads and run for miles, and the first one back had the full use of the shower — an incentive that naturally increased the pace of the run, but it was no fun being tail-end Charlie.

"Right then! Next one." The command came from Les's office. We stood in the changing room awaiting our turn to be weighed. It was my turn next. "Strip off then, down to your underpants."

"I haven't got any underpants, Mr Douglas." I had never had underpants. I was lucky enough to have pants and hardly knew what underpants looked like.

"Then strip to your birthday suit."

"I haven't got a suit, Mr Douglas."

"Look, Bryan! I want to weigh you, so take off your trunks. You've nothing to be ashamed of." I reluctantly shed my last remaining piece of clothing and stood in front of him. Les glanced at me idly then said, "Well, I suppose you have nothing to be proud of either. Now, jump on the scale, Bryan." I did as I was instructed. "Six stone seven pounds when soaking wet," shouted Les. Then he added. "I think we'll have to get some flesh on your bones, Bryan, because I've seen more meat on a butcher's knife."

Les's assistant Harold Lawson noted the weight and wrote it in his diary. As a young lad this was rather an embarrassing experience, but as I realised later, there was neither harm nor malice in these off-the-cuff remarks, it was just the way of men communicating with each other. These asides were straight from the shoulder — there was no pussy-footing about with Les. If you could not accept it, then you were obviously not the right material for the job in hand. He adopted a bold, hard-man front — after all, he used to be a professional boxer — whereas Harold Lawson was entirely different. I think Harold had just been an amateur. He was a very nice man to get on with and all the boys without exception loved him. He always had a happy smile and cheery remarks to make like, "How are you little Tigers today? Are you all ready for a good workout?"

Harold lived on the other side of the River Mersey in a lovely rural village called Bidston, which was on quite a high hill. From this vantage point you could look north-east across to the River Mersey and beyond. By turning around to face south-west you could see the mountains of North Wales. On top of the hill was Bidston Observatory and also an old but active artillery piece. At one o'clock precisely every day the Bidston Gun would fire. It was a recognised time signal. The gun's report would be heard throughout Merseyside, the Wirral peninsula and North Wales, and people would check their timepieces by it. Harold would often take us boys on trips to Bidston. We would get the electric train from James Street station in Liverpool and travel underneath the River Mersey, across Wirral then get off at Bidston. Harold forked out for the fares andkept us in check and interested all the time.

Rambling over the hills, he would point out interesting plants and wildlife to us. If he came across his friends or neighbours he would introduce us. Harold was a mature man and lived with his mother, without children of his own — I don't think that he was ever married. He seemed genuinely fond of us boys and not in a nasty way. I often think back on those days, with a mature and enlightened mind, and I have no reason to think that what Harold did for us scallywags was for any ulterior reason. He lived far away from the dereliction of Liverpool and he genuinely wanted to give us blitz kids a view of a different life to the one we lived in.

The first boxing contest I took part in was in the south end of the city and was certainly an experience. It was quite a big hall, packed with people, mostly parents and families of the contestants. All the boys of our club were in the big changing room with boys of the other club, and we looked around apprehensively at the other contestants, trying to ascertain who was to be our combatant.

"Keep yourselves toned up now, shadow box, keep moving and keep warm." These words of encouragement to the nervous boys came from Les.

"O'Reilly versus Jones!" The shout came through the opened door to the arena. Les went out with Jones by his side draped in an old dressing gown that was twice his size. There were shouts of encouragement from within the dressing room to the two combatants as they left. The rest of the room would listen to the roars of the crowd and wonder who had won. Schoolboys' amateur boxing is limited to three rounds of one and a half minutes with a break between rounds of half a minute. It doesn't seem a long time until you are actually out there in the boxing ring. But young boys are impetuous and they never stop once the bell has gone: they don't stand back and study their opponent like professionals do, they simply tear into one another and their energy is quickly spent. The door opened and O'Reilly and Jones reappeared, steaming and covered in sweat; anxious pals were asking eagerly "Did you win?"

134

"MacManus versus Kelly!" came the order through the doorway. I then got my first glimpse of my protagonist. He wasn't as tall as me but he had plenty of muscle.

"Come on, Bryan, put this around you," said Les, wrapping the king size and sweaty dressing gown around me and fastening up the sweaty gloves on my bandaged fists that he had just removed from Jones. "Follow me close now, Bryan. I don't want you running off."

I left the changing room to the well-wishing of my teammates, then entered the main arena. The seating area and floor space were packed to capacity, with the crowd applauding the entrance of the gladiators. I followed Les, who was to act as my second into the ring; my opponent was already in the opposite corner. The referee called both boxers to the centre of the ring.

"Now, I want a good clean fight, and when I say break, you break. Keep your hands up and no hitting below the belt, do you understand me?" We both nodded agreement. "Right, then go back to your corners." Back in my corner Les gave me my last instructions.

"Now keep your hands up, watch your guard and keep poking out your left jab."

"Seconds out! Round one!" said the referee, and the boxers' seconds left the ring.

"Ding! Ding!" went the bell. The young adversaries were now ready for battle, moving towards each other in earnest fashion. We both waded in with both hands pumping away like steam-driven pistons. Defence was forgotten in the heat of the moment, since scoring hits on your opponent's head was of paramount importance. The roar of the crowd was like a drug, inducing you to keep moving. My heart pumped madly and my chest was burning.

"Ding! Ding!" The referee stepped in between us and sent us to our respective corners. Les was now in the ring with a stool for me to sit on, a bottle of water and a bucket. He mopped my sweating face and body then put the water bottle to my mouth.

"Don't swallow it, just swill your mouth out and spit it into the bucket. You're doing OK but keep your guard up," he said.

"Seconds out! Round two!"

"Ding! Ding!" God that was quick, I thought, but the second round was much as the first, with both of us hammering away at each other, and it never seemed to end. The skills that I had been taught had all been forgotten, with no time to think tactics, just to hit out.

"Ding! Ding!" Oh thank God for that, I thought. Back in the corner Les was working on my cut lip and telling me that I had nobody to beat, that I was in front on points, that all I had to do was keep poking out my left jab and guarding my jaw with my right.

"Seconds out! Last round!"

"Ding! Ding!" The referee called us both to the centre of the ring to touch gloves as was customary for the last round. No sooner had we touched gloves than we were at it again like demented dervishes, but we were obviously tiring by now and once or twice the referee had to intervene to separate us from a clinch.

136

"Go on, Bryan, use your straight left, boy!" The strong masculine voice could be heard over the general roar of the crowd, and it lifted me to greater effort — and so it should have done, it was the voice of my dad.

"Ding! Ding!" Oh what a relief, it was all over. Both boxers embraced each other then we went to our corners, where our gloves were removed from our steaming fists.

The referee was now conferring with the two judges at the ringside, then he returned with a slip of paper and beckoned us to the centre of the ring. Holding each of us by the hand he made his announcement: "My Lords, Ladies and Gentlemen. The judges have found it difficult to make a decision on the outcome of this well-fought contest, therefore as referee I have to make the decision with my casting vote. And the winner is MacManus." He raised MacManus's hand aloft as the victor, the crowd erupted with roars of approval and roars of disapproval depending on which camp they belonged to. Well, I had now been initiated into the world of amateur pugilism. Les told me that I had done well, while wiping the blood and snot from my sore and swollen face. I was once again draped in the king size dressing gown to add my own body moisture to the cocktail of sweat and grime that it had already soaked up.

I seemed to lose more fights on casting votes than anybody else, at least many more than I won. One of the highlights of my short boxing career was when I fought at the Liverpool Boxing Stadium, where I lost again on a casting vote, but the experience was well worth it, and of course Dad was there to cheer me on. Mother used to play hell with Dad when I came back with swollen lips.

"Oh that's terrible! Look at his face, it's all swollen."

"Don't worry, Peggy, it will soon go down. Anyway, the other fellow looks a damn sight worse."

"It shouldn't be allowed, shouldn't be allowed," Mam would say.

CHAPTER
TWENTY-ONE

The General Election

It was now 1945. The war in Europe was over and won and there was now to be a general election throughout Britain. The wartime coalition government led by Winston Churchill was now at the end of its term, but Churchill was still in control under a caretaker government. The last general election had been back in 1937 when I was a five-year-old child. As a young lad of thirteen I was very excited about this coming election, having listened to my dad talking about it and the newspapers were full of it. The war was still raging in the Far East and had taken a back seat in the media, while politics, politicians and the election were the main talking points. British servicemen still overseas who wanted to vote (and that was the vast majority of them) were able to vote by proxy.

"Who are you going to vote for, Dad, Conservative, Liberal, or Labour?" I asked.

"Well, son, I am a working man therefore I will vote for the party that represents the working man."

"Which one is that, Dad?"

"Labour, son, Labour, and they are going to win this election. They are going to sweep to power throughout the country."

"Why don't you vote Conservative, Dad?"

"Because myself and the rest of the working class have nothing to conserve but our families. We barely get enough to exist on as it is."

"What about the Liberals, Dad, why don't you vote for them?"

"Well, they are not much better than the Tories, son . . . not much better than the Tories." Dad had a habit of repeating a statement to add emphasis.

"And who are the Tories, Dad?"

"That's the name given to the Conservatives long ago. It means robbers, son . . . robbers," he repeated yet again.

"Do all working-class people vote Labour, Dad?"

"No, lad, unfortunately they don't. Some of them think they are a cut above the rest, perhaps it's because they have a soft job, or they work for a small firm and don't want to vote Labour in case their boss were to find out. And of course there are those who are that friggin thick in the head they haven't got the intelligence to know any better." I could see that Dad was getting himself wound up, through answering my inquisitive questions, because he didn't normally swear. He was always optimistic about the future, wanting a better life for his children and future grandchildren. In his eyes the key to this end was socialism, which means a society working together and for each other just like a very large family. Now isn't that a wonderful dream and certainly something that we should all strive for? Or is it too optimistic, too utopian, too far-fetched? Well, not to me it isn't, and like my father before me I shall continue to dream the good dream until I can dream no more.

To us working-class kids the build-up to the election was a complete change from the normal run of life. My mates, both boys and girls, were as enthusiastic as I was. We would be in a group and cheer every time a car covered in Labour posters and with a loudspeaker attached went by. We also had a simple political song that we sang continually, especially when the Conservatives were within earshot:

Cheer up, Labour, you're voted everywhere.
We'll beat the robbing Torics
And crush them to despair,
And if they ask for mercy
Mercy won't be there,
So cheer up. Labour, you're voted everywhere.

"I've another job for you, Bryan, but you had better put your old rags on so as not to upset your mother."

"What's that, Dad?"

"While your mother is at the shops, get a bucket of limewash made up and paint Vote Labour on as many blank walls as you can find — but make sure that the scuffers don't spot you, OK son?"

"Oh that's great, Dad! I know where there are plenty of blank walls."

"Good lad. Make the letters as big as possible . . . AS BIG AS POSSIBLE," he shouted.

Dad used to take me to political meetings of both Labour and Conservative candidates that were held in school halls. There he would have his say and question the speakers on the bench, and he was not afraid to open his mouth. After all the campaigning and political argument was finished polling day came, and with it hordes of people released from six years of total war converged on the polling booths. There was no television, with swingometers or all the paraphernalia that we take for normal in today's elections. There was just the simple wireless. Some people would stay up late to listen intently as the results trickled in, but the majority went to bed — after all, it was work in the morning and they had trams to catch and the optimistic hopefuls among them said it was a foregone conclusion and that Labour would romp it, and they were right.

"Labour in power with an overwhelming landslide victory. Clement Attlee the new prime minister." These were the headlines the following morning in the national press. Clement Attlee had been the deputy prime minister to Winston Churchill in the coalition government during the war. Now he had ousted Churchill and was prime minister himself.

The country was almost bankrupt after the bloodshed of war. There was a colossal task in front of the new Labour administration of revitalising and rebuilding the nation. But the hopes of Labour were not to last, for in the following general election, in 1951, the Conservatives and the war leader were back in power. Ironically, Clement Attlee started life as a Conservative when he was at Oxford. But his experiences working in an East End social settlement were enough to convert him to socialism. As I see it, the capitalists controlled the newspapers and were responsible for the defeat of Labour in the 1951 election because the vast majority of people who read the papers are gullible and accept headlincs as gospel. They have not been educated to a standard which will enable them to seek the truth by analysing and criticising the reportage in depth, but just enough to read and accept the blatant headlines. It would be another thirteen years of Conservative misrule before Labour would return to power once more.

CHAPTER
TWENTY-TWO

Leaving School

I never officially left school. I just did not return after
the summer holiday break of 1945, so I suppose I can
say that I left school when I was in my thirteenth year.
I don't remember a great deal about school because I
never learned very much. I don't blame the teachers for
that — the fact is that it was a difficult period for trying
to educate children, coupled with the fact that I was
not academically bright. I cannot remember taking
examinations, but perhaps I did and failed them. Nor
do I remember being questioned about my ambitions in
life, although a man came from the juvenile
employment service and asked me what I would like to
do when I left school and showed me pictures of men
performing various crafts for me to select from. There
was no possibility of staying on at school or going to
another establishment for higher education — this was
it, my schooling was complete. The one picture that
pleased me was of a man assembling what seemed to be
drainage pipes. This was about the height of my
aspirations. I asked the man, "What is he doing, Zir?"

The man replied, "He's a plumber."

I said, "I would like to do that sort of job." It somehow appealed to my hands-on approach to life. I cannot remember what the other pictures were all about. The man took note of this and scribbled something into his book, but I was never given an apprenticeship as a plumber, nor did I ever get an interview for that sort of job. I was given various jobs by the youth employment service and I found a couple myself in the local paper, but I was never offered an apprenticeship. Yet twelve years later and by pure chance I found myself associated with the trade that I had first selected as a kid.

Barratt's in London Road was my first job. It was a gents' outfitters, next to the Legs of Man public house. My duties were brushing the floor, polishing brasses, dusting shelves, running errands and making tea. My wages were seventeen shillings and sixpence per week, with the promise that it would be increased to twenty shillings after Christmas provided I showed promise and was satisfactory. I had just turned fourteen years of age. The shop was owned by two Jewish gentlemen who mostly sat in a little office enclosed in glass talking to each other and at the same time keeping a watchful eye on me and making sure I was kept busy. I could never hear what they were talking about, I just watched their mouths opening and closing. They were like goldfish in a glass bowl gasping for air. I was not allowed to enter their command module — it was sacrosanct. If I wanted something I had to attract their attention by waving my arms, then either one or the other of them would come out of their chamber and talk to me. The

145

shop was frequented mostly by merchant seamen or American servicemen with plenty of money in their wallets. When a potential customer made his way into the shop one of the goldfish would leap from his glass bowl and with a mincing gait and a sickly smile on his wrinkled face approach the unsuspecting victim.

"Good morning, Sir! What would it be that you are interested in?" The predator would beam at his victim, clasping his well-manicured hands, rubbing them one over the other in a wringing fashion. In answer to the victim's question the predator replied, "Yes sir, we do make made-to-measure suits, and we have a wonderful range of the latest materials in stock. Do you have anything particular in mind, Sir? Blue, grey, brown, pinstripe, herring-bone, plain?" He would take the victim towards the shelves stacked out with rolls of differing suiting materials, which the victim would fondle before selecting one. The smiling predator would take the length of cloth selected and unroll it on the long polished table in the centre of the shop floor. "Yes, I think you have made an excellent choice, Sir. This shade of blue will enhance your own natural body colour and excellent dark hair, and of course herring-bone is all the fashion."

"Which style do you think would suit me best?" said the pleased victim.

"Well, you have a good physique and are nice and slim so for you it would have to be a double-breasted suit, Sir. Single-breasted are for the less athletic and more portly types, and of course that definitely isn't you, Sir."

"Oh, thank you!" responded the victim. "Could you tell me how much it will cost, and how long it will take you to make it?"

"For you, Sir, with this choice of top-grade material, that would be seven pounds nineteen shillings and sixpence, and I can have it made up and ready for you to collect in a fortnight's time, would that suffice, Sir?"

"Oh no! I'm afraid that's much too long to wait. You see my ship will be sailing next Tuesday on the evening tide."

"Oh dear! Oh dear! Well I'm sure I could hurry up my tailor to produce the finished goods in time for your departure, but of course I know that he will want to charge me an extra fee for this service, which will be somewhere in the region of two pounds."

"That's quite all right by me so long as it will be ready and I can pick the suit up before I sail," said the victim. The predator continually rubbed his hands gleefully and exuded his sickly smile throughout this verbal interchange.

"Right then, Sir, we had better waste no more time and get on with the important task of taking your vital measurements." Removing his measuring tape from around his neck he proceeded to his task. "I observe that you dress on the right, Sir, is that correct?" The sailor nodded in agreement, the predator then scribbled on his order pad as he took the measurements and spoke to himself. "Inside leg, 32 inches, waist 34 inches, chest 38 inches." On completing the order he ripped off a copy and handed it to the victim. "Right,

Sir, that will be nine pounds nineteen shillings and sixpence."

The victim handed a ten pound note to the predator, then said, "Keep the change and thank you very much and I'll see you next week."

"Thank you, Sir! Thank you very much, Sir, and good day to you, Sir!" The fawning predator returned to his goldfish bowl, adjusted his paperwork and put the money in his cash box. Turning to me, without the sickly smile, he said: "Now go along to my tailor in Byron Street, give him this cloth and these dimensions and tell him that I want the suit in the normal way, that is in three days' time, and collect the Raglan overcoats that I ordered yesterday, and be quick about it."

Receiving my first week's wages was very exciting. It was on the Saturday evening when the shop closed. I had Sunday off and a half-day on Wednesday. I usually walked home to save the tram fare. I liked walking and was used to it and I saw no sense in queuing for slow-moving tramcars. When I got home I handed the seventeen shillings and sixpence to my mother, who was absolutely delighted. She then handed me back two shillings and sixpence for pocket money and fares.

Over Christmas I had been talking to other kids who had recently left school and we were comparing wages and so on. I learned from them that a factory that made cigarettes, cigars and snuff was looking for boys. When the Christmas holiday was over I went along, was interviewed and got a job. I then gave my notice at Barratt's and they asked me why I was leaving. I told them that I had another job that gave me more money and Saturday afternoon off. I wanted Saturday afternoon clear so that I could go and watch Liverpool Football Club play at home. The Barratt boys were none too pleased about my sudden departure and intimated that I should have given them more notice. They also hinted that they had a right not to pay me my week's wages that were held in hand.

"If you don't pay me my week in hand, Mister Barratt, I'll bring me dad to see you and he's a docker."

"I didn't say I was not paying you, I just said I had a right not to. Now, if you wait a moment I'll sort out your money and cards." I thought that if I mentioned that Dad was a docker it would do the trick — Liverpool dockers had a reputation for standing for no nonsense and being tough with it.

Copes Tobacco Products in Seymore Street was my next venture. I worked in the canteen with a band of jolly women from whom I took some stick, mainly because I was young and innocent. They would say things to me with obvious sexual overtones that I did not fully understand, but apart from that they treated me courteously. My jobs came under the heading of a general factotum. The work was mostly outside the canteen but associated with it, sweeping a long cobbled driveway, peeling potatoes and carrots in a hand-turned machine with a rough interior. It was winter and very cold outside. I would be standing under a lean-to turning the handle of the potato peeler; at ten o'clock in the morning one of the women would call me in for a tea break. Oh, was I thankful for it! "Come in out of the cold, my love, and get yourself warm." I didn't have to be asked twice. We all sat in a warm and cosy room, where the women made toast by holding thick slices of bread with a long toasting fork in front of the gas fire.

"Here you are, love, get stuck into this tea and toast." The women were forever jangling and trying to bring me into the conversation.

"What's your name again, son?"

"Bryan," I said.

"Oh! that's a nice name. I've got a son named Bryan," said one of the women.

"Here you are, Bryan, have some more toast and put a bit of cheese on it. You need feeding up, there's nothing of you, and watch how you walk over those gratings in the yard, you could fall down the gaps and vanish." They would all have a good laugh at my expense, but there was no malice intended. They were just good-humoured Liverpool women and hard-working mothers themselves.

I had to go into the factory on occasions and walk through the production areas to individual offices delivering trays loaded with tea in pots, with cups and saucers and biscuits. The first thing that struck me was the powerful smell of tobacco. I would pass girls sitting in lonely wooden stalls and quietly separating tobacco leaves from their stalks. I would see wonderful machines for making cigarettes and packaging them, experiences and sights that were all new to me. Then I would see the contrasting working conditions as I entered wood-panelled and plush offices and gaze on company directors in smart suits and wearing gold watches and gold rings on their fingers.

150

"Oh, you must be the new boy! You're late, you're supposed to be here at eleven o'clock sharp. Put the tray down on that table over there and buck up your ideas, my boy, or you'll find yourself out of a job." On my return to the canteen I told the ladies what had transpired.

"Oh, take no notice of that miserable old sod, love! He probably never got his leg over this morning, that's his problem."

As it was a tobacco factory the management was so concerned about theft that we were all searched when we left the factory at knocking-off time. But despite the brief body search for both men and women, there was still pilfering of tobacco. I would walk home with mates my own age and some lads a few years older and wiser. On the way they would be lighting up cigarettes they had stolen and joke about how they had concealed them — never in their pockets, but down their socks, up their backs or under their caps. I was continually offered cigarettes by them but never fell foul to the evil weed. Yet I was no angel. I soon learned a few tricks from my peers and took advantage of it. My mother, who liked her ciggies, was the grateful beneficiary of my stealth, albeit in a timid and tremulous way. She would show her gratitude but couldn't hide her anxiety.

"Be very careful, Bryan. Watch you don't get caught. I don't want to have to take you to court, and whatever you do, don't mention a word of it to your father."

I eventually moved on from Copes, as I felt that I was not doing a man's job there. When people asked me what I worked at I would have to say I'm a canteen lad or something of that nature, which didn't do my self-esteem much good. But I have nothing but praise for the women who worked there, because they treated me as if I was their own son.

On my frequent journeys to town I would often come across a live band, mostly playing outside the T.J. Hughes departmental store in London Road. The sound of their popular music would reverberate throughout the area. It was vibrant and the women shoppers loved it — I too would often be compelled to stop and admire them. They mostly shuffled along the gutters, five in all, dressed in old army uniforms with their greatcoats buttoned up to their necks to keep out the winter cold. They wore an assortment of headgear, berets, peaked caps and glengarries. On their hands they wore mittens to combat the freezing-cold weather, and on their feet were well-polished and sturdy ammunition boots. There was a piano accordionist, a saxophonist, a trombonist and a big-bass drummer. The big bass drum had no doubt seen better days for it only had one skinned side to it, and painted on the edge of the skin in smart black letters were the words "Liverpool Ex-Servicemen's Band". It was fitting that the big bass drum had only one side to it because the drummer had only one arm. On their left breasts the musicians proudly wore their army campaign medals. The fifth member of this musical troupe would walk along the pavement edge singing in unison with the music of the band.

"I've got youuuuu under my skin . . . I've got youuuuu deep in the heart of me." He would then break from the refrain and go into a tap-dancing routine, rata ta ta, rata ta ta, rata ta ta, rata ta ta. He would then continue with the popular ballad, and at the end thrust out towards his admiring public an old German coal-scuttle steel helmet. The pennies, halfpennies and farthings would be willingly gifted and the clinkety clink as they made contact with the cold steel was sweet music to the chilled ears of the talented musicians.

A pitiful sight that I often came across in town was a man who seemed to be a victim of the First World War — he appeared too old to have been a victim of the Second World War. His legs had been amputated well above the knee and he would sit on a square of wooden board that was bolted to an old pair of roller skates. The assembly was probably 4 inches off the ground, and with a stumpy piece of wood in each hand he would propel himself rapidly along the pavement. Everybody knew that he was coming because of the noise of the bare iron wheels on the flagstones. When he came to the pavement edge he would shoot off and speed across the road, and on reaching the other side he would throw his bodyweight backwards to lift the front skates, then he would lift the back of his trolley onto the opposite pavement. This was done very quickly and with great coordination of mind and upper body strength.

Another pitiful sight was a man who didn't have a nose. He always wore a mask across the centre of his face which was fastened around his ears with elastic. And yet another sight was a young woman who had one leg much shorter than the other, and who walked around with a huge boot on her short leg to balance her up.

Buckingham's Furniture Manufacturers was my third job. The firm existed in and around Kempston Street. I say this because although the company had a purpose-built building, where cabinet-makers would assemble Swedish furniture from pre-packed kits, it also owned a string of dilapidated and uninhabited houses, which at one time had been quite high-class terraced residences. Now the houses were a beehive of activity, producing three-piece suites, chairs, tables and so on. I did a multitude of odd jobs, assisting tradesmen in their daily tasks. Sometimes I would help the chair-makers who produced a lot of wooden chairs for schools. It was good to see how the legs were turned on a lathe and how the wooden seats were made, then how the whole assembly was put together and varnished. The smell of fish glue would be ever-present as it simmered in pots suspended in containers of boiling water. I would sometimes watch the upholsterers produce a wonderful piece of soft furnishing. I learned how to throw the finished product carefully onto my head then carry it across a quiet road to the firm's showroom. I always marvelled at the upholsterers who would take a handful of sharp iron tacks and throw them into their open mouths. Then they would manipulate them with their tongues to bring them rapidly one at a time to their lips where they would pick them off, place them with great dexterity onto the fabric they were working on, then clout them into the woodwork in quick succession. Needless to say, they never smoked or talked while they were at work, producing what to me were wonderful works of art. The company also owned a few dilapidated houses which they rented out and which were always in need of repair. To this end they employed a handyman and gave him a basement lock-up underneath the showroom. I would also assist the handyman in his endeavours to put things right. He was given the firm's transport to carry his tools and materials about the complex. The hand cart was lopsided because the leaf spring on one side was weaker than the spring on the other, and the handyman didn't know how to remedy it, so he compensated for the problem by loading the cart unevenly, which meant that material and tools would constantly fall off into the road. We would attend to badly needed repairs in some of the rented-out properties. I remember, for instance, his attempt to repair a large hole in a bedroom wall where the plaster had fallen off. He used black mortar for the job and the finish was diabolical. Yet the old lady of the house never complained — she was glad that the hole was no longer there. Another time he repaired a leaking lead pipe by peeling back some of the lead, making the hole larger, then putting a match stick into it, finally folding the lead back into place and applying a hot trowel.

"That should hold the water back for a while," he told me. The following week we were at the same address again to repair the same job.

One bitterly cold winter's day our task was to paint the roller shutter doors of a garage belonging to the company. The garage was on the fringe of the

Buckingham empire, on the corner of Craven Street and Islington. It was most fortunate for both of us that a minute's walk away in Islington was a cosy retreat, a haven, a place that you could relax in warmth for the price, of a cup of tea. It was a double-fronted shop run by one man without any assistance whatsoever, neither male nor female. The man had recently been demobilised from the Army Catering Corps, and with his bounty and catering expertise he had decided to go into business on his own. He opened what is known in the Liverpool jargon as a "coke room", which has nothing to do with the well-known American fizzy drink.

In the middle of the large room stood a pot-bellied heating stove on a stone pad, which burned coke. Rising from the stove was an iron flue pipe which disappeared into the ceiling above it, then reappeared on the first floor, rose upwards and disappeared through the first-floor ceiling until it made its way through the roof space from where it found its way outside. How do I know this, you may ask? The answer is quite simple: I helped Andy Mann one day to botch the joints up with mastic compound to stop the lethal carbon monoxide flue gases escaping into the building and thereby gassing all the owner's customers. This sort of work in the building trade is known as a "foreigner", and is always paid with a "back hander". At the back of the stove stood a scuttle that was always kept full of coke. The fire itself was a lethal thing — if you got too close to it it could burn the flesh off you. This was central heating at its very simplest and most cost-effective — and if I may deviate for a moment to quote that most famous Liverpool funnyman Ken Dodd, whose most important possession is his prominent teeth, they "are very good for central eating".

The pot-bellied stove, along with the folding tables and wooden forms, were all government surplus, and indeed a lot of other things were too. This was the period of vast government surplus sell-offs. This popular café was always crowded and there was a never-ending queue at the counter. The smell of grilled kippers always pervaded the air. A kipper and a piece of dry bread cost two pence, half a kipper and half a slice of bread cost one penny, or you could have a pint mug of all-in soup, which would cost one and a half pence. The all-in soup would be simmering away all the time that the shop was open to business and, as its name implies, it was made from everything that was humanly edible, and was both nutritious and delicious. Though from time to time the consistency of its flavour might vary, its colour never changed in the slightest: it was a regulation regimental khaki. Scalding hot tea constantly brewed in two five-gallon tea urns. A packet of tea would be emptied into a deep and fine mesh sieve that would hang inside the urn, boiling water poured onto the tea and saccharin and milk powder would then be added to the brew. Well before the urn in use was empty the second urn would be made operational — there was never a delay. No sugar was provided so you took the tea as it came from the piping-hot urn and in a penny-a-pint mug: what more could you ask for? The

157

clientele were a hotch-potch mixture of non-working and working-class society, roughnecks, ne'er-do-wells, ragamuffins, nomarks, and scallywags like myself. I felt content and at ease to be among them. They were all human beings and each and every one of them had a personal story that was locked up inside their confused heads, which perhaps one day they would manage to download and tell to the whole world.

"Now you carry on painting that door, kid. I'm nipping round the corner for a quick cuppa tea and a warm. If the gaffa appears tell him I've just nipped back to the lock-up for some turps, OK?" I carried on as instructed, painting the door in a horizontal direction starting at the top. It was hellish cold. My fingers were freezing and my feet were like blocks of ice. I could have done with an overcoat but I didn't possess one. The cold was affecting the paint, which was becoming semi-frozen and hard to apply to the metal door. After what seemed like an eternity, but was probably only half an hour, Andy Mann reappeared.

"Anybody come round, kid?" he enquired.

"No," I replied.

"OK, then off you go for a cuppa and don't be too long."

The warmth of the café as I entered was unbelievable. I joined the queue of dishevelled customers and awaited my turn to be gratified.

"A mug of soup, please!" I handed over my three-halfpence and grasped the hot and steaming mug with both hands, then made my way towards a vacant seat facing the window. Seated in front of me in the window bay were the five members of the ex-servicemen's band. They must have arrived just before me because they looked cold and were rubbing their hands together to help the circulation. The one with the German coal-scuttle helmet was just emptying the contents on the café table and arranging the proceeds into five equal amounts, mostly pennies and halfpennies, with the occasional threepenny bit. These men were wealthy celebrities compared to the other customers in the café and were the focus of envious eyes. They were eating a full meal of a whole kipper with an extra slice of bread, and they had a mug of soup each and a cup of tea. I sat there closely studying them and wishing that I could play a musical instrument and hit the big time as they had, so I could be independent and not have to slave for others.

"Ah, come on, kid! We've got work to do." It was Andy Mann shouting through the half-open door.

"I 'aven't finished drinking me soup yet!" I protested.

"Well, bring it with you, he won't mind."

"I'll be there in a minute!" I answered.

"Who's that?" asked the one-armed drummer.

"He's me gaffer," I replied.

"We've got to get this door finished by half-past four," said Andy Mann. "So you had better get stuck into it, kid, 'cos it's my turn to have a cuppa."

"Ha, wacker! Leave the poor kid alone. He's only just come in, can't you see he's shivering with the cold?" It was the singer-cum-tap-dancer wearing his coal-scuttle helmet who was opening up. Andy Mann never responded to these remarks. When he saw the group of five musicians leering at him, he just turned from the door and left.

"You stay for as long as you like, son," said the trombonist.

"You look half-starved, son. Here, go and get yourself a kipper and a couple of chucks of bread," said the saxophonist, handing me a threepenny bit.

"Thanks, mister," I said and hurried to the counter. This was probably the first kipper I ever tasted and it was nice: I've liked kippers ever since. There wasn't much left of it when I had finished, as most of the bones had been devoured as well. When I rose to leave I got jocular remarks and well-wishes from the musicians.

"If you have any trouble with your gaffer, kid, you come straight back here and let us know, we'll sort him out for yea."

"Oh, I see you finally came back then! Now perhaps you'll do a bit of work," said Andy. The painting of the door had hardly progressed from the last time I had left it. So with renewed effort I got stuck in, but instead of being painstaking I just splashed the paint on as fast as I could. I finished the door in no time at all but it left a lot to be desired. Nipping around to the café I rejoined the queue; by this time the musicians had gone back to their late afternoon performance.

"What are you doing here?" said a surprised Andy Mann.

"Same as you, drinking tea," I countered.

"But what about the door?" he questioned.

"I've finished it," I replied.

"Good lad," he said. "I'll nip around and have a look." I stayed in the café for a good half-hour, taking my time supping tea and relaxing. I was in a rebellious mood now that I knew that I had the backing of the ex-servicemen's band.

Andy Mann did not return so I went around to see him. He was really getting stuck into that door and rapidly covering all the places that I had missed. "Right kid, that's about enough for today. Let's load up and be off." That was all he had to say to me.

A couple of weeks later my employment with Buckingham's came to a close: I think Andy Mann had something to do with it. But it did not affect me in any way because I knew there were plenty of other menial jobs for young scallywags like myself, so I simply moved on to pastures new.

The City Mineral Water Company was my next taste of work experience. It was situated in Kensington Street, close to my home. I was classed as a driver's mate, a job I liked because we travelled around Merseyside and North Wales on deliveries. The City Mineral, as it was termed, bottled mineral waters, lemonade, orangeade and various other soft drinks. They also bottled Guinness and other beers that were delivered in barrels from their respective brewers. The company buildings formed a quadrangle. Some were single storey and some were two-storeyed. One two-storey building housed the brewing vats, where the company produced its own brand of alcoholic drinks. Some of these huge uncovered round vats would foam as the brew went through its fermenting stage. Others would not foam because the brew was settling down. It was reputed that the substantial rat population in this area was quite partial to a drop or two of this tasty alcoholic liquid. It was also said that during the hours of darkness when the workers had returned to their homes and the factory was peaceful, families of rats would come out to play in the brewery, congregating on the roof rafters above the vats and then climbing onto the broad rims of the vats. Because of over-indulgence, a number of rats would lose their balance and topple unceremoniously into the foaming liquid. I have seen the brewer fishing them out the following morning with a net attached to a long pole. I would watch him with a look of astonishment on my face, my mouth agape and my eyes as big as saucers. The brewer noticed me watching this grisly spectacle.

"Don't you worry about it, son, the more rats that drown in the ale the fewer there are to drink it, and some of them I can't fish out, they've gone straight to the bottom. Anyway, it's good for the brew, it adds flavour and distinction." Then he added, "Some breweries throw a sheep's head into the vat for the same reason. You never know what you're drinking, son, or eating for that matter."

I was speechless and horrified. Until then I had been a kid who would eat and drink anything without question, but this experience opened my mind to some of the realities of life.

The firm had a fleet of trucks for delivering beverages to retail outlets and individual homes. Some had diesel or petrol engines and some were battery-operated. Every morning we lads would be appointed to go on a certain truck. We had no option — it could be because the driver requested us, or it was the whim of the yard foreman. I didn't mind which truck I went on so long as I got out of the yard, since if you were not appointed to a truck you got a job inside the bottling plant. Here you would have to assist women and girls for the most part, but sometimes men on the washing, bottling or labelling machinery. One of the few men who worked there sticks out in my memory.

He was probably in his early thirties, tall and gaunt, quiet and uncommunicative, hardworking and humourless, yet everybody had the greatest respect for him. After a while I learned why: he had been a prisoner of the Japanese in the Far East and suffered for three years under their brutal regime of ill-treatment, slave labour and starvation. After learning this I too became sympathetic towards him, and an admirer of his dedication towards his work, and am sure that to the company who employed him he was regarded as a model worker.

Once you were selected for a lorry you had to help load it with crates of beers, soft drinks and also barrels of ales. The loading of beer barrels would be done in the yard from a loading bay, but loading with crates was done from the exit door of the bottle store that stood in the narrow confines of Kensington Street. The checker would stand just inside the store with his clipboard and pen and tell us what was required to be loaded onto the delivery lorry. One of the driver's young assistants would start loading his sack truck with five crates full of various bottled beers, then push them outside onto the narrow pavement. Here the driver would load them onto the lorry, and a third youth on the back of the lorry would start stacking the crates firmly against the headboard. The checker would stand just inside the doorway of the store, vigilantly watchful and ticking off the crates from his list as they went past him. There was no room on the narrow pavement for him to stand. In case a bottle was accidentally broken, there were always odd crates of various brands of ales in the storehouse. If you did break a bottle you removed the broken glass and swapped it for a full bottle.

"Now, lad, do as I told you. Don't forget the hidden bottle trick," said the driver.

"OK," I replied. This was the practice of half-inching (pinching) a bottle every time you brought out five crates. The method was to place a bottle of ale horizontally between the two dozen bottles in the fourth crate that you brought out on your sack truck, to make twenty-five bottles instead of twenty-four. You just had to keep your eye on the checker as you were doing this trick, making sure that as you passed him he ticked off another five crates on his clipboard. The driver stood on the pavement and always lifted the top two crates onto his lorry, which was hard going, but it concealed the hidden bottle. By adopting this method of petty pilfering, a fully loaded lorry could have as many as forty half-inched bottles on board. Obviously this meant that there were empty crates lying around the store house, but these were disposed of by other drivers who were awaiting their turn to load up and do the hidden bottle trick. I was usually given about four bottles of this contraband at the end of the day, and as I was not inclined to drink I took it home and gave it to my father.

"Where did you get these from, son?" he asked.

"My driver gave them to me," I replied.

"Hope they're not stolen," he said with a questioning look in his eyes but with a sly smirk on his ruddy face. Then with a cheeky wink he would say, "Anyway it tastes genuine enough to me. Good lad, and don't let me catch you drinking any of it."

Some runs on the lorries were preferred above others by the young lads, and of course they had their preferred drivers. The city deliveries were hard work because there were too many drops within a small area and a lot of heavy barrels were involved. These would be dropped off the lorries onto bean bags, then lowered into the cellars of pubs, clubs, restaurants and hotels. Deliveries into suburbs of Merseyside such as Crosby, Formby, Maghull and Southport were favoured because these were long trips. But the favourite was under the Mersey Tunnel across the Wirral peninsula and into North Wales — this was like being on holiday. The next favourite was delivering to regular domestic customers in the more well-to-do areas of the city. There were two drawbacks to this, though. First, it was all day Saturday working, which meant I couldn't go to the match. Secondly, it was by battery-powered delivery trucks that slowed down as the day wore on, until eventually we stopped altogether and had to be towed back to the depot. The good thing about it was that many customers were quite generous and gave me monetary tips.

In the summer the company organised a free day out to Blackpool for all its employees. We left the brewery one sunny Sunday morning and travelled in two luxury charabancs. The company had provided free booze and soft drinks but we had to take our own sandwiches. It wasn't long before the bottles were being offered around even though it was early morning. By lunchtime the happy workers on their free day out were in high spirits and singing their heads off. When we reached Blackpool the crowd dispersed in small groups after being told what time we were due to return. I went with the young lads to the funfair and tower, while most of the adults headed for the nearest bars — Yates was their favourite watering hole. It was a good day out but quite tiring, especially for the drinkers who returned to the charabanc the worse for wear. When they eventually staggered aboard most of them immediately fell asleep; not a word nor a song left their lips, which made for a peaceful journey home.

The sound made by partitioned wooden crates filled with bottles as they were manfully thrown onto the back of the lorries and then stacked in columns was particularly pleasing to my ears. Also the rhythmic rattle of a fully laden vehicle as it moved off was to me very pleasing. I found that segmented crates of full

166

bottles of beer gave a sound of deep contentment as they were manfully thrown about on the backs of the lorries, whereas the loading of unsegmented crates gave a quite different sound, still contented and happy but more chirpy. Returning crates filled with discharged bottles gave another distinct sound, but this was an empty, dispirited and lonely sound devoid of any soul, but there was still an undercurrent of happiness for they knew that when they were returned to the depot and washed, sterilised and recharged with alcoholic beverages, then their spirits would rise once again.

I do not think that the industry uses segmented wooden beer crates any more — I never see them around. And of course very few bottles are used nowadays. The industry seems to be geared to throw-away cans packed tightly into throw-away cardboard cartons. That is eternal progress but with it has gone the happy chatter of beer bottles and the wooden solidity of a beer crate, the whole ensemble when in movement creating a symphony of happiness.

But after some time I once again became youthfully bored with this work of ceaseless liquid replenishment and was goaded and convinced by my peers that the grass is indeed very much greener on the other side of that distant hill. So I bade my farewells to my contemporaries and excitedly ventured forth once more.

A coffee warehouse in Vernon Street was my next port of call, though in reality this was more than a warehouse. The company imported coffee beans, then roasted, ground and blended them. Having done that they packed the ground coffee into five-pound tins, which were sealed and then parcelled up into packs of six. Most of this coffee was part of a government contract to keep overseas troops happy. In a much smaller capacity, they also packaged tea. This was done in a separate and more secure part of the building. The majority of my time was spent unloading truckloads of raw coffee beans, which was done with the aid of a hand winch securely bolted to a purpose-built wooden platform on the top floor of the warehouse and 8 feet above its deck.

The winch was an iron machine with a central drum, around which was a wire cable with a hook and a rope sling. The driver of the delivery truck would place four hundredweight bags of beans into the sling, then four of us youths, two standing each side of the winch, would turn the bare steel handles attached to a crank wheel — the handles were diametrically opposed to each other. When two people were pulling on their handle the other two were pushing on theirs, which evened out the torque on the drum. This action would revolve the crank wheel and through a gearing system would ultimately turn the cable drum, which would begin to wind in the cable and lift the loaded sling. This was a very laborious and energy-sapping task. When the sling had reached the top floor of the warehouse it would be dragged inboard by two other youths and the sling unloaded. The winch would then be turned in the reverse direction, which was quite easy, but then the process of lifting would start all over again. The youths who had unloaded the beans would trolley them into the depths of the warehouse, then stack them up to reach the ceiling. The six youths would periodically alternate these jobs to ease the boredom and balance out the expenditure of energy. It was really gruelling work. We would look down at the delivery truck and try to assess how many more lifts we had to do before it was unloaded.

A hard, mean-looking, and work-worn overseer with the countenance of a bloodthirsty bull terrier would constantly stand over us and urge us on to greater efforts. At ten o'clock we got a ten-minute respite and dashed off to the nearest coke room. When we returned we got a rollicking, even though we were only five minutes over.

"Where the fuck have you lot been? When I say ten fucking minutes I mean ten fucking minutes. The trouble with you fucking lot today is you don't know that you're fucking well born."

Everybody took their ear-bashing without stopping or answering back. We just manned our positions on the winch and continued where we had left off. After a while the palms of our hands became very tender and blistered through constant friction with the unprotected cranking handle.

"Now listen, you fucking lot. If you want any fucking dinner then you had better finish unloading this fucking wagon first. The carter can't hang around all night for you fucking lot, he's got work to do." Nobody dared answer him or look at his ugly red face. We were stirred on more by our hunger than by his coarse remarks, and by one o'clock we had finished bringing up the last sling. "Good lads. You did well. I knew you'd see fucking sense. Now don't forget I want you back here at one fucking thirty sharp."

We sat in the coke room munching away ravenously on cheese or corned beef sarnies and noisily slurping away at our mugs of tea-urn tea. We were all in a rebellious mood and there was talk between us of mutiny, of sabotage and revenge. It was just idle talk. We had no set plan but it helped us to combat this hated and loathsome individual. It was one thirty-five when we returned to our tasks at the warehouse. We were now a spiritually unified body, but I was beginning to realise that the grass was not greener over the other side of the hill, at any rate not this particular hill; in fact there was no grass here at all. Waiting for us was the overpowering and dominating overseer, and not only that but there was another wagonload of coffee beans to be unloaded: "Right! You lads now, you have all had a fucking good break, and no doubt have replenished your fucking greedy stomachs. With all that renewed energy inside you, you can fucking well start unloading this fucking wagon, and I want it done by five o'fucking clock."

As we stood on the winch platform pulling our guts out we cursed among ourselves. During spells in our labours we would look at the winch hatefully, and suggest to one another the possibility of fouling up its mechanism. The winch was a simple but robust machine, with no electrics involved. We were just inexperienced youths with no mechanical knowledge, and so we could never hope to foul up the energy-sapping monster. But just thinking and talking about it strengthened our camaraderie and raised our moral courage against the foul-mouthed capitalist lackey.

"If we did manage to sabotage the winch, it wouldn't help," said one of the lads.

"Why?" said another.

"Because we would have to carry the bags up the spiral staircase one at a time."

"Blimey! Never thought of that," was the chorus of voices from the rest of us.

Some days there would be no deliveries at all, so we six youths would be split into smaller groups and distributed throughout the warehouse. The raw beans, of which there were many varieties, came mostly from South America. Bags of selected beans would be fed into a chute on the top floor, then gravitate to the next floor. Here they would be blended and roasted in large gas-fired ovens, a process that generated very pleasing smells. After roasting, the beans would be fed downwards to the next floor, where they would be ground, bagged and temporarily stored. The ground coffee would then be placed into hoppers and gravitate to the first floor, where it would be tinned and parcelled up, ready for dispatch. From this floor the parcels of tinned coffee would be placed on a chute and glide down to the ground floor. At various points in this process youthful labour would be used to full advantage. But whatever jobs we were allocated to it was heaven compared to winding the dreaded winch.

171

At least it was gratifying to understand that everything gravitated from the top floor to the dispatch bay thanks to our pulling power. And as the finished parcels glided down the final chute unaided, I thought it's me and the lads who are doing that with our kinetic energy.

In the 1940s standards of food hygiene were at a low ebb from what I could see. For instance, on the second floor where the coffee was ground, the worn-out machinery spilled out so much coffee that it lay on the floor 2in thick. People constantly walked through it wearing their outdoor footwear, dropping their fag ends into it and even clearing their noses and throats and yockering into it. This did not concern me at the time. I was new here and this was the system. Sooner or later it would all be cleared up, I thought, and every weekend it was — I was on the cleaning party. Ground coffee was swept off the highest points of the grinding machines, then it was brushed up into nice big piles on the floor. The coffee was then shovelled into a sieve that was clipped to a hessian bag, and when the bag was full it was tied and labelled and stacked with the other bags of ground coffee. The sieved contents of fag ends, bits of wire and congealed unidentifiables were dumped and the sieving process continued until all the spillage had been recycled. This coffee eventually went down the hoppers to the tin-filling machines on the first floor, then down the chute to the dispatch bay on the ground floor, awaiting delivery to indiscriminate and grateful customers.

Just before Christmas the five other youths and I were told that our services were no longer required.

172

The company had fulfilled its government contract, made its profit and therefore we were made redundant. The term redundant was something I would come across time and time again as I made my way through the learning curve of industrial life. There was no compensation in this case, just a two-hour warning period on a Friday afternoon.

Beacons Products on the Waterloo Road was a company operated by two ex-Royal Navy officers, who worked in the building on all aspects of production. There was also a sort of semi-sleeping partner whom we only saw occasionally. He was the principal financier who worked mainly from home and brought in the sales orders. The premises were yet another old warehouse, just like the one I had recently left in Vernon Street. I learned to my dismay that it also had a hand-operated winch on the top floor, but when jobs are scarce beggars cannot be choosers. It also had a spiral staircase made out of wrought and cast-iron, that rose from the bottom to the top of the warehouse. There were already three youths working in the warehouse, making me the fourth. The company also employed a lorry-driver-cum-handyman and general factotum. This driver had been recently demobilised from the army, having served in North Africa with the British Eighth Army under Field Marshal Montgomery.

The two men who ran the company, the lorry driver and the other three youths were good to work with — perhaps the grass was now looking greener. The company's product was scouring powder, made from caustic soda, ash and chalk. These raw materials were delivered to the warehouse from the nearby docks by horse-drawn carts. Two heavy shire-horses would pull the carts. One would be harnessed between the shafts, and the other would be harnessed directly in front of the first in such a way that its pulling power was utilised to the full. This part of the dock road was the Waterloo Road. It was cobbled or made of stone sets and was the main thoroughfare for dock traffic, with scores of carts pulled by horses and heavily laden with merchandise travelling north and south along its length. Steam-driven traction engines with boilers burning anthracite were also commonplace. They were considerably quieter except for their "puff-puff-puff" as they accelerated. The electric overhead railway ran the full length of Liverpool docks on the west side of the dock road and adjacent to the high brick and granite dock walls. Underneath the overhead railway there were two sets of railway lines, which also ran the full length of the docks, a distance I believe of 10 miles. On these tracks slow-moving steam freight trains would constantly move from dock to dock carrying a large brass bell in front of the engine. Traffic and pedestrians were always aware of the approach of these trains by the persistent clanging of their bells brought about by the movement of the train. And at busy junctions a man would step from the footplate and walk in front of the engine carrying red and green flags.

From the top floor of the warehouse and looking down and forwards you could have a panoramic view of the whole industrial scene. Seagoing freighters in what

174

was then Clarence Dock, which was immediately opposite the warehouse, could be seen discharging their cargoes or loading up for their next voyage. When we had a delivery of soda, ash or chalk, whatever work that was taking place in the production of scouring powder would stop immediately. Everybody would give a hand to unload the wagon either on the winch or dragging the bags inboard and stacking them up. It really was a matter of all hands to the pumps — even the management gave a hand. There was no cursing, nor foul language, but everything was done quietly and smoothly, and thanks to the ex-Royal Navy men on board everything was shipshape. Having unloaded the wagon and sent the carter on his way, we would all go below and relax with a nice mug of tea, which we took turns to pay for, but the boss would always pay for more than his share. The coke room was on the corner of the next block. It was frequented mostly by dockers, carters, fitters and grease monkeys. We would normally go in with a tray and collect seven pint mugs of steaming tea; the proprietor knew where we came from and never argued about the mugs.

One day while we had all been unloading on the top floor, a family of black warehouse rats had taken the opportunity to help themselves to our packets of cheese sandwiches that had been left on a bench top. The warehouse was plagued with rats and the boss had forgotten to warn us about them. He apologised and treated us all to replacements from the coke room, and with this gesture his already high rating with us went even higher. From then on we protected our sandwiches by suspending them from the ceiling hooks by lengths of string. As in Vernon Street, natural gravitational forces were used to get the raw materials from the top floor of the warehouse to the finished and packed product on the ground floor dispatch bay. Chalk and soda ash would be fed into a trough which had a horizontally rotating mixing blade. From there the mix would be fed through hoppers into a filling machine, and we would put a round cardboard carton under the machine and fill it with scouring powder. Then another machine would roll a metal cap onto the open end, and a dozen cartons would be wrapped in brown paper and sealed with sticky tape. It was a simple operation, but the navy men had not quite ironed out the gremlins in the mixing machinery. Every now and again the machinery would stop because the free-flowing powder had compacted somewhere in the system. I felt sorry for the navy men, climbing up ladders with spanners in their hands, unbolting flanges and tapping with hammers on parts of the machinery then eventually shovelling out the mixture from the starting trough. The rest of the crew would of course be taking orders and helping to find and clear the blockage. When this happened, which was quite frequently, we would all end up looking like snowmen and our hair would be caked in the stuff.

"Here you are, Bryan, go and get some tea." The chief engineer gave me these instructions, together with a shilling piece. It was a merciful instruction for we were all parched from breathing in the throat-clogging powder. The good point about scouring powder was

176

when the spillage was cleared up and recycled at least it was not for human consumption. On occasions, I would go with the lorry driver on deliveries to retail outlets around the Merseyside area and as far afield as Manchester. I liked doing this because I could ask him questions about the recent war which was probably one of my main interests in my young life. Sometimes we called at his home, if we were passing near by, and I met his family and we'd sit down for a quick cup of tea and a chat. I was a very thin lad without any obvious muscle, but I was extremely fit. I used to cycle to work, which was quite easy because it was mainly downhill and involved a lot of effortless free-wheeling, provided I spread my legs wide and avoided the flying pedals. But cycling back home in the evening was a different matter. Although the distance was no more than 2 miles, there were some very steep hills to climb. I put together and maintained the bike myself, using any odd pieces that I happened to come across. It was a fixed wheel and gearless but reliable bone-shaker of a steed, devoid of class or pedigree, but it seldom let me down and it knew exactly where home was.

I was travelling home one night after leaving work and as I pedalled up the steep incline of Saint Domingo Vale I saw a horse lying on its side in the middle of the road. It had been pulling a coal cart and I think the steep incline was too much for its heart to take. Still tethered to the shafts by its harness, it was not quite dead and the forlorn coal merchant was kneeling by its side. He looked a pathetic sight. His face was black with coaldust but beneath his eyes and down his cheeks were white lines where the coal dust had been washed away by his tears. I stood around for a short while and witnessed the vet putting paid to the poor animal with a humane killer. He then helped the carter to remove the horse's harness and throw it onto the back of the cart which was half-loaded with sacks of coal. I peddled away towards home wondering how the unfortunate coal merchant would be able to continue his rounds without his faithful companion. Horses are such loyal and hard-working creatures, bending to man's every command, but man takes them for granted until tragedy strikes and he realises that his dumb animal also has a soul.

Taylor's Provision Merchants, Soho Road, were essentially wholesale potato merchants, but they would provide other produce as well. They had two lorries, two drivers, two driver's mates and the proprietor who classed himself as the yard foreman. I was surprised to see that the other driver's mate was somebody I recognised but didn't like — he happened to live in the next street to ours, Keeble Street. He was nearly two years older than me and was a renowned bully. He knew that I had gone to a Catholic school so I was a prime target for his religious hatred. He was a Protestant and he had obviously acquired his anti-Catholic phobia from his parents, who came from Glasgow, a city with a tremendous religious divide. At any opportunity he would sidle over to me and break into a one-sided conversation.

"Ah! 'ave ye 'ad it in yet eh! 'ave ye, bet ye 'avant?" A self-gratified grin would cross his horrible pockmarked face. "I bet ye 'avant got a fireman's helmet, 'av yea?" I didn't like this sort of talk. I was young and inexperienced and feelings of a sexual nature were only just beginning to manifest themselves in me. "I'm giving my notice in at the end of the week, I'm sick of this place," was his final comment, before he was called away by his driver, which was very pleasing to my ears.

Truckloads of potatoes would be delivered to the merchant in bulk, either straight from the farmer's field or perhaps imported from abroad. If they were straight from a farmer they would come in high open-backed lorries and would be tipped into wooden-sided and open-fronted bins in the yard. From here they would be shovelled into hessian sacks and weighed, then the sacks would be tied at the corners, producing two grasping ears. The one-hundredweight sacks of spuds would then be stacked into piles according to what class of spud it was, reds, whites, King Edwards, Irish, Jersey. This work was normally done after all deliveries for the day had been completed, and was a filler for time that was still available. Soon after eight o'clock in the morning we would start to load up the lorries. This had to be done one at a time because the entire labour force was needed to load one lorry, two men throwing the sacks of spuds onto the back of the lorry, one grasping the ears and the other the bottom. The man on the lorry would use a sack truck to pick up and position the sacks, starting at the headboard. This was hard manual work, and it seemed to get harder as the grass got greener, but there was more to come. Once on the road we would commence on a round of regular customers, greengrocers, chip shops, hotels, restaurants. Everybody ate potatoes daily in one form or another, potatoes being Britain's staple diet. All greengrocers had huge potato bins made of wood which started about 3ft off the ground and ended at the ceiling. The front of these bins had removable wooden slats to hold the potatoes in place, and the bottom slat was wide with an arch cut into it to allow the potatoes to be scooped out. When we made our delivery we would carry the bags of potatoes into the shop on our shoulders and empty them into the bin. As the bin filled up we would replace the wooden slats until eventually we would have to climb a ladder to reach the top of the bin. Shops would have about three or four bins, with a different variety of potatoes in each. Cabbages were another main vegetable, and were huge, dark-green and leafy, not like the pale leafless and plastic coated things we eat today. Most of the retail outlets would get their vegetables from another supplier or collect themselves from the main wholesale market. Delivering to chip shops was much easier since they normally stored their potatoes in the cellar or in their back yards.

And on the subject of chips it is worth remembering that it wasn't always fish that went with chips. Another commodity that was a lot cheaper and which the Lancashire working class were accustomed to was tripe, made from the stomach of an ox. There were other delicacies as well — pigs' feet, known as trotters, and pigs' heads would also be on display in the chip-shop window. Then there was brawn, a red-coloured meaty product that melted on your chips and to me tasted quite nice. Some of our deliveries would be to cargo ships tied up in docks and preparing to sail. They would order a complete mix of vegetables and fruits, which we would collect from Cazneau Street wholesale vegetable market. The apples and pears we collected were always in open-topped boxes and when we delivered them to the ship they were always considerably lighter. During the war there was no shortage of bread, but after the war was won grain became scarce one year, which resulted in the rationing of bread. The same happened with potatoes. I remember one customer, who had a large tripe and chips shop, took drastic measures to beat the potato shortage. He was well-to-do and had a big house with a large front garden so he hired our labour through the company and we proceeded to dig a huge clamp pit in the front lawn. He also ordered two lorryloads of spuds and when we had finished digging the pit we lined it with straw, then commenced emptying the sacks of spuds into it and continued pouring potatoes into it until we had built it up, just like a pyramid. The pit was about 8ft wide by 2ft deep and it ran the whole length of his garden. When all the potatoes were unbagged we covered the pyramid with a thick layer of straw, which in turn was covered with the earth spoil from the excavated pit. I remember that careful attention was taken to add a number of ventilation exits to the top of the clamp pit by adding vertical tufts of straw and surrounding them with spoil. I believe that this is the traditional method of storing potatoes throughout the winter.

Moving on yet again in my quest for better grazing, my next work experience was at the rodent disinfestation department of Liverpool Corporation Public Health in St John's Lane. I was interviewed by the head of the department, Mr Mitchell, a big, heavy and pleasant man who had his own office. In the general office was Mr Mitchell's middle-aged secretary, Miss Prim. There was also a Mr Stamp, a general clerk. I recall that Mr Stamp was always preening himself, cutting his nails, paring the cuticles back and brushing himself down. There was also a Mr Dalzell, known as the canal-boat inspector.

In the rear assembly room stood a long oak table with about eight chairs either side. In the middle of the table was a box separated into compartments marked in, out, pending. The disinfestation officers would assemble here every morning, along with their supervisor. Each officer was responsible for the disinfestation of rodents, both rats and mice, from one particular area of the city, and the supervisor would have a roaming commission, in order to keep his beady eye on them. In an airless, windowless and unventilated storeroom, which had a heavy steel security door, worked a tall and proud ex-Royal Marine. The heavy door gave the impression that the room must at one time have been a strongroom for valuables, before the Corporation took it over. The ex-marine was in control of rodent baits and poisons and it was his job to prepare the mix each day as requested. The disinfestation officers would fill in requisition slips and the storeman would provide what they needed. There were different types of rodent bait, but the one I remember easily was called sausage rusks. There were also different types of poisons, arsenic and Warfarin being two that I recall.

The storeman had a good pedigree yet he was constantly away from work with ill health, and his complexion was anything but rosy. I have always been health conscious, probably because of my childhood experience of diphtheria. I did my best to steer clear of dust and unpleasant smells, which is one of the reasons I never smoked cigarettes. But on my way out of the office I always had to pass the poisons store, with its noxious and nauseating smells. Yet the ex-Royal Marine who spent his war years breathing clean, cool and fresh salty air, was not aware of the harmful environment he was working and dying in.

The office staff had pensionable and permanent jobs, and they wore smart civilian attire. The second grade of operative was the area inspector. The storeman was one of these, as was the van driver, whom I would assist. They all wore uniforms. Two other men formed the base of this pyramid, Charlie and his "hoppo", Mick — the lowly paid drain inspectors, whose rank I shared.

Every weekday morning I would report to the office at eight o'clock and sign the attendance book along with everybody else except Mr Mitchell. The driver would receive various daily instructions from the area officer's supervisor and/or Mr Mitchell. I would diligently follow the driver to his van and perform any task that he was entitled to give me.

Letters and postcards addressed to the Public Health Department would ultimately find their way to St John's Lane, where they would be put in the appropriate in-tray. Each morning the area inspectors would peruse the correspondence, letters from citizens of the city who had spotted the offending creatures and were none too happy about their experiences. The inspectors were obliged to follow up all complaints and would compile a rota of their intended visits for that day and leave it in their out-tray. No one had a car, not even Mr Mitchell, and so they would pay for public transport and hope to be reimbursed, if they could prove that their journeys were really necessary.

Our first port of call was a small quiet depot in Eaton Street off Vauxhall Road. The driver had a key to the gate which he passed to me and said, "Open the door, lad. By the way, what is your name?" I told him. "My name's Mr Wilson, but you can call me George," he said. I was to learn that George had once been a chauffeur for the Lord Mayor but because of economic cut-backs he had been demoted to his present miserable post. He wore a uniform and peaked cap, kept himself impeccably smart and considered himself far too important to soil his hands, even to the point of refusing to open the depot door. I loaded the van with bait boxes for rats and mice, together with wire rat cages, smoke machines and a white enamel bucket with a lid. The bucket contained dead rats that had been

184

caught over a wide area of Liverpool, each with a label attached to one of their hind legs to indicate precisely which area they had been caught in. Each rat was wrapped in a white muslin bag soaked in paraffin oil.

Our next stop was the Port Health Authority's office by the Princes Dock entrance. I would take the bucket inside and collect more dead rats — these had been caught on ships that had docked recently in Liverpool. The Port Health Authority had its own independent workforce. We now travelled to the School of Hygiene and Medicine situated on the corner of Mount Pleasant and Oxford Street. Here I would lay out the rats on a marble slab in the laboratory as indicated by an assistant technician. The School of Hygiene would open up the rats, take out various organs and examine them under a microscope, looking for signs of plague, scarlet fever, diphtheria, smallpox and other debilitating diseases. As the rats were labelled the authorities were able to pinpoint the key areas or the name of the ship that had brought them to this country. I would leave the laboratory with the remains of the last delivery and place them in the back of the van.

When I returned to the van George would be reading his *Daily Express*, supping tea from a thermos flask and nibbling dainty little three-corner sandwiches that his wife had prepared and placed into his lunch box together with a small piece of cake and an apple. This was the cue that I had been waiting for, since at my interview Mr Mitchell had advised me to bring sandwiches and a flask of tea to work because breaktimes were not regular, and mostly taken by the

185

side of the road. Mother had made me thick cheese sarnies, thick as door steps, and we didn't possess a flask so I took a glass lemonade bottle full of tea. The sarnies were nice but the tea was now lukewarm.

When I finished my break George said, "You had better fill in the log now, Bryan."

"What's that?" I replied. George indicated a large diary in the glove compartment of the van.

"That book there. You will find there is a page for every day in the year. Find today's and fill it in, indicating every call we make, why we came, what time we came and what time we left. Here's a pen and don't lose it."

I didn't expect to have to do clerical work: writing was not my best subject, though come to think of it nothing was my best subject and when it came to spelling, well I just couldn't. I was just a tall, gawky and very strong lad. But I would attempt it — I had to, it was part of my job. I couldn't expect the driver to do it, as he had enough to do just driving the van.

"Here, you had better do it in pencil first so I can see what your writing is like," said George. I picked up the pencil and hesitantly wrote in the diary while George looked over my shoulder: St John's Lane . . . de offiss 9oclock till hafpast 9 pikkin up ordiz.

"Well, you got St John's Lane right, how did you manage it?"

"I saw it on the name plate," I answered.

"Look now, I'll write the first call in the diary then you'll know how it goes. You know that I shouldn't be doing this, don't you? Mr Mitchell could well look at

186

this diary so you had better improve on your writing and spelling." George wrote the first call: St John's Lane . . . the office . . . 0900 till 0930 . . . collecting correspondence.

I thought that was very decent of him, saving me from a lot of bother and from then onwards I wrote each call in pencil and when my spelling mistakes had been pointed out by George I corrected them with a pen.

We now went to an address where the drain inspectors Charlie and Mick were waiting for us. As instructed, I heaved a heavy and greasy wooden box out of the van and placed it at Charlie's feet: it was a smoke machine.

"Is there any oily waste in there?" said Charlie to me.

"What's that?" I asked. Charlie opened the box.

"Lucky for you, son, this is what it is. The machine is no bleedin use without it. Now you make sure that there is always plenty of it in the box."

"Where do I get it from?" I said.

"It's in the bleedin depot. You can't miss it, ask any bleeder, they'll tell you."

"All right, son?" enquired Charlie's hoppo. In a friendly manner, Mick added. "Don't worry, kid, you'll get used to it." Both men were about the same age, in their forties. Charlie was more responsible than Mick and was quite conscientious. Mick was a likeable rogue with a happy disposition and didn't care if the world ended tomorrow. He rode everywhere on an old and rusting carrier bike, with a redundant kipper box firmly wedged in the carrier. Because of his mobility, he would go shopping on a daily basis, heading for where any decaying and unwanted foodstuffs left over from the markets were dumped. He was well known here for his brazen idiosyncrasy and with great aplomb he would sift through the varied selection of rotting produce and pick out only the finest that were on offer.

When a disinfestation officer visited an address in answer to a complaint of rats being seen on the premises, one of the things he would do was to survey the area outside and look particularly for holes and sunken paving stones. This could indicate that rats were coming up from the sewers via the broken drains. He would then make a request for Charlie and Mick to investigate with a smoke machine, which in effect was just a chamber that burned oily waste and a bellows pump that provided air. Attached to the outlet of the chamber was a flexible hose that would be put around the dried-out S-bend of an outside gully or toilet. The oily waste would be ignited and Mick would start pumping: if smoke escaped from the holes, it would prove that the drains were broken, thereby allowing rats from the sewers to make their way up the broken drain and burrow out into the open. While Mick was pumping Charlie would adopt a more important posture and stride about the external area looking for the first whiff of smoke. "Thar she blows!" Mick would shout on spotting the first column of smoke coming from a hole in the ground, much to the annoyance of the superior Charlie. Subsequently, if the break was on land belonging to the owner of the premises, he would be officially notified of the problem and be given a firm date by which to have the broken drains replaced. If the break was in the back entry or roadway, then the Corporation would have it repaired.

Charlie and Mick would have a number of drains to test each day in various parts of the city, but I noticed that most of them were in areas of poverty and structural neglect. We would try to deliver the smoke machines in advance, which gave us more time to collect them when the test was completed. Rodent bait boxes were delivered to and collected from a wide variety of premises, private dwellings, shops, hospitals, schools and factories. A daily call was at a large Corporation depot in Lune Street, to collect dead rats from inside a tall chimney pot standing on the ground. These rats had been caught alive here in cages that had been lowered into sewer manholes. On retrieval they were killed, then a label was attached to one of their rear legs which identified where and when they were killed. I would collect these specimens for the following day's delivery to the School of Hygiene. At the far end of Lune Street was the public waste incinerator, where I would dispose of unwanted rodent carcasses by tossing them into the furnace.

"You had better give your hands a good wash now, Bryan, because it's dinner time, and you don't want to catch weil's disease, do you?"

"What's that, George?" I asked.

"It's a nasty disease that you can catch from the urine of rats," he informed me. I was not issued with protective clothing, not even a pair of gloves, but then again nobody wore industrial gloves because that was

189

considered real sissy. I used the toilet facilities in Lune Street depot, which could have done with a good clean themselves, and cleansed myself as best I could. After this George would normally find a quiet place and park up, so we could have our midday break and I could bring the logbook up to date with George's knowledgeable assistance.

"No Bryan, you don't spell masheen that way, it's machine." Not only was I learning a new job but I was being educated as well. After lunch we headed for Belmont Road Hospital and the offices of the Chief Medical Officer. "Now smarten yourself up before you go in there," said George. "Take this correspondence with you and hand it in at reception and ask if there is any to collect."

From here we went further down the hospital drive to the Chief Health Inspector's office. Without bothering with reception, I went straight in to Mr Binns himself and swapped correspondence. He was a big powerful man and it was quite daunting to enter his office, not just because of his size but because of his title and the lofty position that he held. He never said much to me: his eyes were mostly fixed on his paperwork and if he did say anything it would be something like, "Make sure that Mr Mitchell gets this letter today, not tomorrow. It's very important, do you understand, young man?"

"Yiss Zir, yiss Mr Binns." On occasions like this we would double back to the office and give the important letter to Mr Mitchell straightaway.

190

We would then head for the depot in Eaton Street, which was always unlocked at this time of day. In the large mess room was a cooking range, a long wooden table and an assortment of chairs. Hanging on the walls were cooking pans, frying pans and an array of cooking implements. On the table were a variety of cracked, handleless and begrimed tea mugs. Summer or winter, the fire was always lit, with people sitting around it supping tea and talking. The people were always the same. First there was Mr Dalzell the canal-boat inspector. Nobody knew exactly what he did for a living, although we did learn that he occasionally walked the Leeds-Liverpool Canal and talked to bargees. These bargees lived their whole lives on the narrow boats, lived, slept, made love, had babies and ultimately died there. It seemed obvious that Mr Dalzell had a keen interest in their public health and safety, not of course through piety, but because of the remuneration he received for doing it. Other frequenters of the mess room were Big Arthur and his little mate Harry. They would just sit, sup and chat with Mr Dalzell. As sewer men, their job was to drop the baited rat cages down the manholes and into the bottom of the sewers, then open up the sewer outlets the following day and see what they had caught: they said they were fishing for runaway fish. Whatever they caught they would kill and bring into the depot, with identifying labels attached.

Mr Dalzell was quite an affable character but he always talked down to his inferiors, and spoke authoritatively on the latest news topics. I didn't know

191

a lot about worldly political things, so I would sit and listen to the dialogue being exchanged between the more informed members of the gathering. What I did learn from these verbal transactions was that although each individual had his own point of view, Mr Dalzell would always win them over to his way of thinking. He voted Tory, as did Mr Wilson, and so I came to the conclusion that working-class people who considered themselves a cut above the rest of their class voted for the capitalists. Also seated at the table was Charlie, who didn't usually take much part in these endless discussions; he was sociable enough with the others, but unlike them he was not a time-waster. As soon as he had finished his lunch he would retire to his workshop, which was next door to the mess. Here he would spend the rest of the working day making and repairing wooden bait boxes and wire rat cages.

George would normally walk around to the Corporation Ambulance Depot in Gascoyne Street. He felt more at home with the ambulance drivers, who all wore smart uniforms and peaked caps like himself, and of course his van was washed and maintained there.

I would sit at the far end of the table eating the remains of my door-step sarnies and sipping my cold tea. "Here, son, don't drink that, it's cold. Have some of this, it's piping hot." Before I could refuse, a huge cracked mug was filled with steaming tea and thrust in front of me. It was Arthur who made the gesture and I thanked him for it. I looked at the grimy mug and observed the stains and dried rivulets of tea from the previous drinker adhering to its chipped exterior.

"Here he is, here's the lad," said Arthur as a figure was seen outside the mess room window. This was Mick, resting his carrier bike against the wall. He walked into the mess with a beaming grin on his rugged face, and carrying his kipper box in front of him which he plonked onto the wooden table. The political dialogue that had been taking place was now suspended, for jovial couldn't-care-less Mick was now the centre of attention.

"Got any good pickings today, Mick?" asked Harry.

"I've got some of the finest selection of Jersey tomatoes, Spanish onions, and giant mushrooms, also a nice handful of stringy bacon." Mick reached up for the large iron frying pan begrimed with the greasy residue of yesterday's cooking, and placed it on the open coke fire. He then threw the bacon quite casually into the sizzling pan, he cut up the onions and threw them in too, followed by the tomatoes and mushrooms, which he washed under the outside tap because they were looking a bit unhealthy. He then poured some hot water from the kettle onto the concoction and stirred it thoroughly; the smell was quite appetising. When Mick was satisfied with his culinary masterpiece he removed the frying pan from the fire and slammed it onto an old newspaper that rested on the table top.

"Do you fancy a sample, lads?" said Mick to the assembled audience of curious onlookers. But there were no immediate takers to his hospitality.

"I might try a small taste later," said Harry.

"There won't be any left later," said Mick, "If you want some then get stuck in now."

"You won't eat all that by yourself will you?" asked Mr Dalzell.

"Too bleedin true I will! I've been grafting all day, not sitting here drinking tea like you lot, and besides I haven't eaten for a long time." Mick took down a stale loaf of bread that had been resting on a high shelf and proceeded to cut himself a thick slice. "Blimey, this is hard," he said.

"I should think it is," said Arthur. "It's been up there over a week — it's a wonder the rats haven't found it." Unperturbed, Mick waded into his meal and softened up the hard bread by soaking it up in the fatty juices.

Arthur and Harry were an enigma to me. They were not under the jurisdiction of Mr Mitchell, or Mr Dalzell for that matter; in point of fact Mr Dalzell was also an enigma: his starting place was known and his finishing place was known, but the middle bit was a mystery to all. Arthur and Harry spent a good deal of time here in Eaton Street Depot. They came just after midday, sat around drinking, eating, and talking until at five o'clock they headed home. As I saw it, their only reason for coming here was to deliver their dead rats, in order that I could collect them. In the mornings they obviously reported to some obscure depot, where they received their daily instructions. Then they lifted up a quantity of manholes, caught their quota of rats and that was it — they then retired to the comforts of Eaton Street. The exception to this rule was Fridays, when they had to go early to pick up their wages. I was told that on Fridays Harry's wife was always waiting for him at the pay station, where he would obediently hand over his pay packet. Everybody knew this because Harry's mate Arthur gossiped about it, relishing a feeling of superiority as he retold the story again and again to new and unaccustomed ears.

My duties in the depot were varied. Sometimes I had to label the rats that Arthur and Harry had brought in. If they didn't have the time themselves, I would then place them in individual muslin bags. I would also bag the rats from Lune Street, dip them all in paraffin oil, then place them on a griddle to drain off for the morning delivery. Occasionally, rats from other sources would appear in the yard and I would process them along with the others. I was always kept busy, with instructions from Charlie, sweeping up, washing windows, hanging up Mick's dirty pans.

"Don't wash them, son," Charlie would say to me. "Mick doesn't like them clean, he says it spoils the taste of the grub."

When I returned home from my first day's work Mother enquired about my new job, as mothers do.

"Were your sandwiches all right, Bryan?" she asked.

"Yeah, smashin', Mam," I said.

"Where did you have your lunch?" she asked.

"Eaton Street," I responded.

"You ate in the street?" she questioned.

"No, I ate in the Corporation depot in Eaton Street," I explained.

When Dad came home he was also inquisitive. "You've got a good job there son, a job for life with the Corporation, so long as you keep your nose clean and don't get into trouble."

I could understand Dad's concern for me: he still worked on a casual basis with the Mersey Docks and Harbour Board. You couldn't get much lower than that because if there were no ships entering the Mersey then you didn't have a job but relied on fall-back pay, which was just like being on the dole. To have had a permanent job would have been heaven for Dad.

"You'll never be out of work in that job, son. There will always be rats, they keep coming in on the ships just like immigrants, they multiply faster than you can kill them off."

But I didn't want a job for life and I couldn't see that far in front of me. I was young, I wasn't ambitious, just young and I wanted to know what life was all about. If I stayed in the same secure job for the rest of my life I would never develop my mind or gain worldly experience. I was now nearing eighteen years of age and was looking forward to conscription and worried in case I didn't pass my medical. Dad didn't relish the thought of me being called up for military service and he told me so.

"Look, Bryan," he said, "when you go down for your medical tell them you are a conscientious objector."

"What's that?" I asked.

"Tell them you don't want to join the army."

"But I do want to join the army," I told him.

"Look what happened to your Uncle John," he said.

"Yes but there was a war on then, wasn't there?" I countered.

"There are always bloody wars, and they are caused by the idle rich who get the sons of peasants to do their

196

fighting for them." Dad was now on his soapbox and I could sense the rebellious Irish spirit rising within him. He had good cause to be rebellious and anybody reading Irish history would understand why. He was not an educated man but he was intelligent and he knew what was wrong and what was right. All he was doing was trying to conserve the only things that he possessed and lovingly cherished, and those were his wife and family.

The medical examination board was in town, and packed with eighteen-year-old youths. We sat around in a very large hall waiting for the proceedings to start. The hall was sectioned off by screens into open-fronted booths. The first batch of youths were documented then told to strip off — there was absolutely no privacy in the place. Their clothing was left on the wooden forms they had been sitting on. I was documented along with others in strict alphabetical order, then told to strip off. We then formed a file and queued at the first booth, waiting to be examined by a doctor. I forget how many doctors there were, but each one examined a specific part of your anatomy.

"Bend over and touch your toes," instructed doctor number one. I could feel his hands grasping my buttocks and gently parting them. "Right, stand up!" now he was fondling my testicles. "Right, now move to the next booth."

Here my chest was examined with a stethoscope and my ribs tapped. "Right, move on!"

My eyes were examined next, and then came the oral examination, followed by an examination of my hearing and then reflexes.

Finally came the psychiatrist, who did not examine any part of my body but looked at me deeply with piercing eyes.

"Do you know why you have come here today?" he asked.

"Yiss, Zir, to be examined medically."

"But why?"

"To see if I am fit enough to join the army."

"And are you?"

"Yiss, Zir."

"Good man. Now go and get dressed, then move to the next booth." I struggled to get dressed like everybody else because all our clothes were mixed up by people who had just left or those who had just come. I now went to the final booth.

"Have you a particular preference for an army unit?" As I knew nothing about the army I didn't have a choice.

"No, Zir," I said.

"Was your father in the services?"

"No, Zir."

"Have any of your family been in the services?"

"Yiss, Zir, all of my uncles were in the army."

"Good. Do you know the name of the regiment they served in?"

"No, Zir." I learned later that the army try to put you in a family regiment or one of your choice, and if this is not possible it's left up to the vagaries of the selection board.

Glad that the medical examinations were over and pleased that they found nothing wrong with me, I returned to work to inform Mr Mitchell of my good fortune: I just couldn't wait to join the army.

"How did you get on today, son?" said Dad when he returned from work.

"I passed A1," I gleefully told him.

"Did they say when you would be going?" asked Mam.

"Yiss, in a couple of months' time."

"What about your job?" Dad asked.

"Mr Mitchell said he wants to see me when I return from the army."

"Oh that's nice of him!" said Mam.

"It's nothing to do with being nice, they have to give the lad his job back," said Dad.

CHAPTER
TWENTY-THREE

A Soldier of King George VI

With my call-up papers and a train warrant, I was to report to the number one training battalion, RAOC at Aldershot in Hampshire. Dad was moderately pleased that I had been enlisted into an Army Corps and not into an infantry regiment; he was still thinking of his elder brother John. At that time I didn't know anything about the make-up and complexities of the army, so it didn't make much difference to me. I was in the army and that was all that mattered.

"You'd better find the times of the trains," suggested Dad.

"How do I do that?" I wondered. Travelling by steam train over such a long distance was alien to me, and I didn't know how to go about it: I even struggled to find the place on the map.

"Telephone the station from the telephone box on the corner of Albert Edward Road, by the chemist's, and don't forget to press button "A" when you hear a voice," said Mam.

I had never used a phone in my life — I was breaking new ground all the time. When the person at the other end answered, I completely lost my well-scripted lines, and because of my rapid delivery and strong Liverpool accent, the cultured person at the other end of the phone couldn't understand what I was talking about. I then decided to take the tram to Lime Street station where I could discuss my problem face to face with somebody.

On the morning of 19 January 1950 I said goodbye to Mother and left the family home with just the clothes that I had on my back, and not knowing when I should return. What more did I need? By this evening I would have a new suit, and I couldn't remember the last new suit that I wore. I will admit that I would not be able to select the cut of the cloth, nor the colour of the serge, and of course it would be off the peg. The chances were that it might be brand-new, but then again it might be recycled: I had heard reports that some soldiers were issued with lucky battledress uniforms, whose bullet holes were neatly sewn up again. These were considered lucky on the principle that lightning never strikes twice in the same place.

It's hard for a young man to understand what goes through a mother's mind when a child she has given birth to, brought up and nurtured goes off and leaves her. Mother was never a demonstrative woman, but concealed her feelings from the onlooking world. I never ever remember seeing her shed tears. I had said goodbye to Dad the night before, because I knew he would be up early as usual for work.

"You look after yourself, son, and don't forget to write to your mother," were his parting words to me.

I was a fledgling Liver-Bird fluttering its unaccustomed wings, ready to soar blindly into the beckoning future, unaware of its apparent pitfalls and dangers. A scrawny, pimple-faced and malnourished youth, I was not yet a man. I was not even entitled to vote, and would not be for another three years. I was now a mere kid of eighteen and eager for adventure. I was ready like hundreds of thousands of similar British youths who over six years of bloody conflict had become indoctrinated with vehement fervour and passionate patriotism for the country we loved. We were ready to defend the proud British Empire on which, we were taught at school, "the sun never sets". During geography lessons the teacher would tap with his cane of authority on the red areas of the world map and declare, "This is the British Empire, the greatest empire the world has ever seen." This statement was proudly proclaimed by the impassioned teacher but it didn't mean a lot to us scruffy kids sitting there in our scuffed and unpolished boots, our short trousers and snotty pullovers, although it did make us feel a sense of pride both in ourselves and the country we lived in. "The Empire" was still huge but was beginning to dwindle into obscurity, finally to evolve into the worldwide Commonwealth of Nations.

I caught the No. 10 tram to Lime Street and headed for the station. I had never been on a steam train before, only on an electric one. There were lots of other young men like myself milling around the platform, some saying goodbye to their parents, others to their girlfriends. I took a seat in a compartment where others were already seated, chatting and getting to know each other. Enquiries were made as to who was going where. It transpired that one lad was going to the same place as I was, and he seemed to be well clued up with vital information.

"When we get there they'll give us all kinds of aptitude tests," he knowingly informed me. "Now, what you want to do is to fail the tests, then they'll put you in the Pioneer Corps, and you'll be sent to Chester, which means you will be able to get home every weekend." I took this information on board, but I had no intention of acting on it, and I couldn't understand the mentality of people who neither gave their best to society nor sought to improve themselves. This no-mark who attached himself to me was continually rabbiting on and chain-smoking cigarettes. He told me about the scams he was up to and what a good life he had, only to be interrupted by the army. I was very glad when the train pulled into Euston station and did my best to give him the slip, but he hung on to my tail. It was a bit confusing at the station for us inexperienced travellers because we had to find our way to another station and pick up a connecting train for the final leg of our journey, but somehow or other we made it, despite being apprehensive in case we should miss our connection: the War Office had given us detailed instructions with regards to our journey, together with travel permits, and a warning of the dire consequences of late or non-arrival. Our worst fears soon abated when we found our train waiting in the station. There were very few commuters on it, the bulk of the passengers being young men like myself. We travelled about 30 miles to the south-west of London, and as the train slowed down and pulled into Aldershot station we were aware of military personnel standing on the platform. Aldershot was the renowned military garrison town, and those on the platform were our reception committee. As we alighted from the train it was easy for anyone to distinguish between normal commuters and enlistees, for the commuters hurriedly departed leaving the enlistees standing around like the lost sheep that we were.

"Right, hurry along, you lot, and fall in outside on the station concourse."

This gentle command came from a smart and erect soldier, whose upper tunic sleeves displayed a set of three chevrons. Outside the station stood a number of three-ton army trucks, each with a driver standing beside the lowered tailgate. The sergeant held a clipboard and pad in front of him, pointing to an enlistee who was hanging on to a suitcase.

"Where do you think you are going with your suitcase, laddie, Butlin's holiday camp? If that is correct then you have got on the wrong train." The unfortunate enlistee remained quiet, but subdued titters of laughter came from the others. Now turning his attention from the embarrassed individual to the mocking mass, the sergeant paused in his delivery, gazed upon them as one, then opened his mouth wide and bawled: "There will be absolute quiet in the ranks when I am addressing an individual, is that understood?" He paused again for effect and to let his words sink into their minds, then concluded, "And the answer will be 'yes, Sergeant'."

The now subdued mass mumbled, "Yes, Sergeant."

"I did not hear you. I want you to open your mouths wide and say it again."

"Yes, Sergeant!" was the full-blooded response.

The sergeant then continued with his lecture; looking at his clipboard he said: "When I call your name out, you will come to attention by raising your left foot off the ground then slamming it down again next to your right foot, at the same time bringing your arms directly against the sides of your body, keeping your body erect, looking ahead of you, pulling your shoulders back and tucking your chin in, and at the same time shouting in a clear voice 'Sergeant'. After your name has been called you will seat yourself in the rear of the leading vehicle. Is that quite clear?"

The response was again a full-blooded "Yes, Sergeant!" Our names were bellowed out in strict alphabetical order, and when we sat in the vehicles we had to remember who was in front of us in order to maintain the correct alphabetical sequence. We had been given our very first sample of the army's method, discipline, and regimentation; I for one had no complaints, in fact I loved it. We learned from the lorry drivers that we were the second batch of the day; those from London, the Home Counties and the south were already being processed in the barracks. After us lot from the north of England, would be the final batch from Scotland and Northern Ireland.

The convoy moved off and travelled a matter of a few miles to the mainly timbered Parson's Barracks. Here we were processed, documented and kitted out, and here we would live for two weeks doing very basic training and undergoing aptitude tests. The first thing issued to us was our army number, which we had to memorise immediately: mine was 22324943, and still is. Fifty-two years after putting it onto my mental hard-drive, it is still there. I couldn't erase it if I wanted to and my recycle bin won't accept it. We then entered the quartermaster's store, where a long counter confronted us, lined with storemen and behind them assistants. Behind the assistants were storage shelves and bins from floor to ceiling and travelling the depth of the building. Beyond the last storeman was a clerk with a wad of documents in triplicate known as AF 1157.

The first item issued was a kit bag in which we crammed all the material flung at us in quick succession. Once the storeman had asked our size he flung in two pairs of hobnailed leather boots, and then a pair of plimsolls. After that, size never mattered and you were asked no more questions. You just progressed along the counter and items of equipment and clothing were thrown at you. If it was clothing then the storeman would weigh you up with a professional eye, give a shout to his assistant and the required item of estimated size would be immediately issued to you. The final act was the signing for the goods issued, with a warning that any loss would be reissued and the cost deducted from our pay.

As soon as we had signed we made our way individually to a dormitory in what was termed spider block, a block of three dormitories spread out like the spokes of a wheel with the hub acting as the place where the whole complex performed its ablutions. One-third of the dormitory was occupied with new recruits, who were in varying stages of settling in. I had now to collect my bedding, two half-mattresses, known as biscuits, two sheets, a pillow with case and four blankets. It was now about four o'clock in the afternoon. I hadn't eaten since breakfast time and was really hungry. Everybody else must have been in the same position, since up to now there had been no mention of being issued with food.

The recruits who lived in a dormitory would be known as a platoon, and they would have a platoon corporal as their instructor. The corporal would sleep in the same dormitory but in a small separate annexe. Corporal Decivilianise gave us a long list of verbal instructions:

As soon as you return from the bedding store, you will make your beds. For those of you who have never made a bed before you are permitted to look at mine. You will then unpack your military equipment and place it neatly on your bed. Finally you will disrobe your civilian garb and put it out of sight inside your wardrobe. If you wish we can store it for you, but I would suggest that you take it home with you on your first furlough because you will not be needing it any more. Finally you will dress yourself in your second-best battledress, complete with boots and gaiters. There will be a surprise for the first laddie who can transform himself from a slovenly civilian into something resembling a British soldier. Any questions?

"Yiss, Corporal. Which is the second-best battledress?" I enquired.

"That is a decision that you alone will make, and make it wisely," he warned. I was very keen to see what I would look like dressed as a soldier and wasted no time in complying with the list of instructions received from the corporal.

At this point a sergeant entered the dormitory, spoke to the corporal then left. We were not to know that the sergeant was doing his rounds reminding the platoon corporals of the evening's guard duty. No matter where you are in the British Army, be it at home or abroad, whether in a purpose-built barracks, in tentage or just bivouacking, military guards must be mounted. And Parson's Barracks was no exception.

The dormitory was now full and every bed occupied. It was a hive of activity, with recruits getting to know each other, helping each other and giving each other advice. We were a mixture of British youth from the union of four countries, each of us an individual and a complete stranger to the others. The most notable difference was our accents, Scots, Geordie, Irish, Scouse, Welsh, Cockney, Yorkshire, West Country and a host of others. I was standing by my bed talking to the lad next to me while busily adjusting the straps on my gaiters — I was probably more advanced than the others in transforming my image — when a question was directed at me from the corporal.

"What's your name, laddie?"

"Kelly, Corporal."

"Don't you have a rank?" he asked me.

"Err, what's that, Corporal?"

"You're in the army now. You are not Kelly any more. From now on unless you get promoted you will be known as Private Kelly. Is that understood, Private Kelly?" The rest of the platoon were anxiously watching and listening intently to this verbal intercourse. "And that goes for the rest of you," said the corporal, sweeping his eyes around the sea of stone faces.

"Yiss, Corporal." I answered. He looked me over with a critical eye then proceeded to adjust my beret and tug at my belt.

"Tighten that belt, Private Kelly, and straighten your tie." I quickly complied with his instruction. "Now that's a lot better, and because you are beginning to look something like a soldier I have a surprise for you. You are on guard duty tonight." I hadn't the faintest idea what that meant. "Don't worry, you will not be on your own. There will be twelve of you, all from different platoons." He finished off with the usual line: "Any questions?"

"Yiss, Corporal. What time is dinner?" I was starving, and I think the others in the platoon were glad I asked the question.

"Evening meal will be served between 18.00 and 1830 hours in the main mess hall, but not for you. You will report to the guard room at 17.55 hours. It's near the main gate. You will go dressed as you are now plus your greatcoat, as it gets very cold in the early hours of the morning." Then as a rider he casually said: "Evening meal for the guard will be served in the guard room. You had better take your mess tins, tea mug, and eating irons with you in your small pack. Any questions?" There was silence. I wanted to ask him what this funny way of referring to time was, but I didn't want to show how ignorant I was. So I asked the lads, most of them whom like myself didn't understand, except one chap who had been in the Army Cadet Corps. He explained that it was the twenty-four hour clock, and that the time was now 17.30 and not half past five. I continued with tidying up my bed space then climbed into my greatcoat which had gathered a multitude of creases through lying in the QM stores. There were sympathetic remarks levelled at me from some of my new-found friends because of my misfortune in being selected for guard duty on my first night in the army, but they also commented that they were glad it was not them.

"I would take the gloves if I was you," said my buddy in the next bed. We had been issued with woollen khaki gloves. Thinking that was a good idea I shoved them into my greatcoat pockets and made my way out of the dormitory.

"Best of luck, Scouse!" said my immediate buddy, and the well-wishing continued until I had left the dormitory.

The guard room stood just inside the main entrance. It was a single-storey, wooden building about 30ft by 15ft, with an open veranda at the front where a group of unhappy looking young men, all wearing wrinkly greatcoats, were standing. As I approached a corporal admonished me: he was the guard commander.

"Come along, that man. Step lively and fall in here. Name?"

"Private Kelly, Corporal." He ticked off my name on his clipboard, then the final three guards approached and were treated in the same inimical manner. As the twelve of us rookies stood at ease on the veranda, the corporal did his best to give us the image of soldiers by tugging here and pulling there at our uniforms. We were then issued with pickaxe helves and told to hold them by our sides and steady them with our right hands.

"When the orderly officer appears I will spring you to attention, is that understood?"

"Yes, Corporal," was the answer from a chorus of throats. We then saw a resplendent figure in a well-tailored officer's uniform approaching from the officers' mess, an imposing wooden building on the other side of the road.

"Attennnnn-Shun," bawled the guard commander. The raw guard gave their best interpretation of complying with the command, one lad dropping his pickaxe helve in the excitement of it all. He was immediately reprimanded: "You dozy individual, pick it up!" The orderly officer had now halted 15ft from the assembled ragbag of guards. The corporal, noting this, immediately swivelled about, marched smartly towards the officer, halted with a crash of boots, saluted then bawled: "Regimental guard ready for your inspection, Sir." The officer thanked the corporal, returned his salute in the casual manner that is habitual of officers, then went forward to inspect the guard.

Everybody feared the worst but it was not to be. The young second lieutenant walked along the front and rear of the trembling rookies, turned to the corporal and said in a cultured voice, "Quite a good turn-out considering, corporal."

"Thank you, Sir," replied the corporal. Salutes were exchanged, then the officer returned to his mess. The corporal then approached the guard and read from his clipboard the guards duties: "You will be split into three lots of four. Each group of four will be known as a stag, is that clear?"

"Yes, Corporal."

Moving along the rank the corporal said, "You four are the first stag, you are the second, and you are the third", then he bellowed: "First stag stand fast. Second and third stags left turn into the guard room, quick march." I was on first stag. The corporal briefly went into the guard room then returned. "Left turn! Quick march! Right wheel! Left! Right! Left! Right! Halt!" We halted beside the main entrance where the first of our stag was given his briefing: he was to guard the main gate and not move away from it. He had the luxury of a

212

man-sized sentry box in case it started to rain or snow. "By the left! Quick march! Left! Right! Left! Right!" The rest of us were marched to different points of the barracks and given our instructions, which included being alert at all times, not deserting our post and not meeting up with each other. We were known as prowlers and would be on guard for two hours, and when we were relieved at 20.00 hours we would be marched back to the guard room for dinner. The guard room was bare except for the essentials, one table, four chairs, four iron beds without mattresses. There was a small ablution block at one end and a room with chair, table, phone and the guard commander's iron bed at the other end.

Nobody likes being on guard. It's probably the worst sort of duty you have to endure, and it's a lot worse when at night. I was thankful for the greatcoat, with the collar turned up and buttoned, and was glad that my buddy had reminded me about the gloves. Thinking about it I don't think I had ever had an overcoat or gloves in civvy street — yes, I was better dressed now than I had ever been, I even had underpants and pyjamas. I walked up and down the barracks' roads, occasionally hearing distant music that was probably coming from one of the messes. It was all terribly boring and I was ravenously hungry. I didn't possess a watch and there were no clocks on my travels so it was difficult to gauge the time. The distant sound of heavy boots marching rhythmically towards me was an indication that my period of prowling was coming to a close.

"Guard halt!" The prowler replacing me fell out and I fell in at the corporal's command. The group of four guards were marched around the barracks to relieve the other posts, then we were marched to the guard room.

"Right, lads, you'll find some food and tea in those dixies. Help yourself then relax in those chairs," said the guard commander. It was now turned 20.00 hours.

"At 22.00 hours when number three stag goes on duty, you lot can have the beds, then at 24.00 hours you will be on duty again, is that quite clear?" His words didn't make much impact on our minds but we acknowledged them: our main concern was to satisfy our hunger. We took the lids off the stainless steel dixies. One was a third full of tea, the next was a third full of mashed potatoes and the other contained a quantity of fried sausages and bacon, which had been there for two hours and was absolutely cold. There were subdued mumblings of complaint from two of the guards, who had been used to better things in life, but I and a hungry-looking Scots lad got stuck in and dolloped the uninviting but nourishing food into our mess tins. I greedily ate my fill, swilled it down with cold tea, then relaxed for two hours with my head cushioned into my small pack and resting on the table top. I dozed fitfully, trying to gain some comfort from my awkward position, placing my woollen gloves between the coarse webbing of the small backpack and my face. At 22.00 hours I was wakened from my slumber by the guard commander rousing number three stag with a few choice words of encouragement. The iron beds were now vacant and so I immediately lay down. Although we were lying on the uncovered springs it was more comfortable than sitting on a hard metal chair with my pack under my head and my beret over my eyes to shield them from the electric bulb. I immediately fell into a deep sleep.

"Wakey! Wakey!" I couldn't believe it: I had only just lain down, or so my mind informed me, but in effect it was now 24.00 hours, midnight. We knew the drill now: march to your post, take stock and think of wonderful things in order to pass away two boring hours of your young life. But I didn't really mind, I was an apprentice soldier. I was clothed and fed and next week I'd get paid in full with nowt taken out. These two hours were more boring than the first two, though. I had quickly used up my stock of dreams and was feeling cold and miserable. There wasn't even the sound of distant music to break the monotony. But I was comforted to think that I would soon be relieved from guard duty and could look forward to the dawning of my second day as a national service conscript.

At 06.00 hours the camp bugler sounded reveille, the guard was stood down and dismissed after being told to report back to our billets. The dormitory was already alive with activity, with people travelling to and from their ablutions. My bed was very smart, the sheets and blankets having been made up into a sort of sandwich. "Who did that?" I asked my dormitory buddy.

"The corporal was demonstrating last night how we must make up our beds each morning and as you were on guard duty he used your bed as an example." I was quite pleased with this as the others were now

215

struggling with theirs. Talking to my next-bed buddy I learned that the platoon had spent the previous night listening to the corporal instructing them on how to assemble their webbing equipment, because on today's first parade we would be wearing it.

"Don't worry, Scouse, I'll help you," he said. "You had better look at the rota pinned on the wall, Scouse, and see what job you've got to do in the dormitory," said Bud. My job was to make sure that the fire buckets were full of sand and clean water, also to polish the brasswork on the stirrup pumps. This had to be done every day. "But now get yourself washed and shaved, then change into your denims and we'll go for breakfast. The cook house opens at 07.00 and we're on parade at 08.00." The lure of breakfast and what it had in store was all that I needed to stir me onwards, and in no time I was ready for it.

The dining room was huge, and as we entered the door a lance corporal on duty said, "Take your beret off!"

"I should have warned you about that," said Bud. As we joined the long quick-moving queue of rookies, the smell of food tickled my nostrils. I noticed that the only people wearing headgear were those on duty, which included the cooks and assistants behind the counter. I followed Bud's example and picked up an indented meal tray and held it in front of me as I faced the servery. There was a server for every item of food, which was either placed, flopped, slammed or flicked onto my tray — sausage, egg, bacon, tomato, beans, black pudding. We helped ourselves to bread, butter, jam and tea at the end of the line, while being watched critically by another lance corporal. The dining room was neither particularly noisy nor particularly quiet; there was a mediocre hum of animal contentment coming from the busy mouths of the perpetually hungry youths. I glanced around the room studying the faces and tried to recognise or be recognised. This was day two. I had met a lot of people and was seeing fresh faces all the time, yet I wondered where all the faces I had already seen had gone.

It was now 07.30, and as I left the hall with Bud a voice said, "Put your beret on, laddie." I did as I was told. I was quite happy now that my stomach was full. Back at the dormitory all was haste, beds being made up, cleaning duties performed and webbing equipment donned.

"Come on you lot! We're on parade in fifteen minutes and I don't want any cock-ups. My platoon is always recognised as being the best in the battalion." This was our corporal exhorting us to better things because he didn't want his high standing, whether true or false, to be undermined by us green newcomers. "Right, those who are ready fall in on the road outside and the last one will be on guard duty tonight." This was the army's way of getting the best out of people, by instilling competition and speeding up their responses. I had just experienced a bout of guard duty and knew it would not be my last, but I was certain it would not be tonight. I very quickly completed my rota duties, tidied away my kit, checked my bed space, then fell in on the road wearing my beret, denims, boots, gaiters, belt, cross-straps, ammunition pouches and small backpack. Half the squad were already there, the rest were still inside the dormitory being hurried on by the corporal. Meanwhile, those of us on the road took the opportunity to help each other make final adjustments to our webbing equipment.

Other platoons were forming up on the roadsides, some in physical training kit, others in battledress and others still in denims. The battalion had a strict basic training programme of lectures, film shows, medical inspections, haircuts, marching drills and selection courses. It was obvious that every platoon could not be doing the same thing at the same time, so events were neatly organised into one- or two-hour periods to avoid clashing. All this information was displayed on a roster in each dormitory, and we were all expected to know in advance what the day's programme was and how we should dress for it. The rest of the platoon straggled out and formed up as best they could in three ranks, the last man still struggling with his webbing; everyone else was glad that they were not the worst specimen on parade. The purpose of this parade was to inspect our webbing equipment, but as we did not know any drill movements, the corporal had to cut corners to get this exercise under way. We came forward one at a time for his inspection, criticism and adjustment.

"Take careful note," he said. "You have all been shown how to wear your equipment. I don't want any failings in the future. It is now 08.55 hours: you have five minutes to return to your bed spaces, change into PT kit and return, and your bed spaces will remain as

218

they are now. Fall Out." We dashed away in panic, because nobody had been taught how to fall out properly in the correct military fashion.

After an hour of PT under the guidance of a separate instructor from the Physical Training Corps, we were dismissed for a NAAFI break. During the afternoon there was square bashing and a haircut parade with short back and sides all round by the demon barbers of Parson's Barracks. After the evening meal there was more work, getting the creases out of our uniforms using a simple electric iron and a damp cloth. To ease the burden of waiting our turn for the iron we were taught how to bull our boots to perfection using a method known as spit and polish. The pimples in the leather of the toecaps were eradicated by rubbing with a heated spoon, then boot polish was applied. The art was to make small circular movements across the toecap with a duster wrapped around your forefinger and applying liberal quantities of spit. After many, many hours spread over many, many, days the toecaps started to show signs of metamorphosis. They would adopt a hardened and reflective surface, of which the owner became very proud. Squaddies would compare each other's boots and enquire as to the particular method employed to achieve such brilliance. It was noticed that the instructors had perfect boots, but this was not achieved by their own efforts: this was the labour of others who had been coerced into it, and for such labours the instructors would reward them in the form of light duties. Warrant officers and sergeants also had immaculate boots and uniforms, but this was the work of official batmen.

When at last my turn came to use the iron I seemed to lack concentration — I was listening to a spicy tale being recounted by one of the platoon. Consequently, in pressing my battledress tunic I didn't notice that the damp cloth I was using had a large hole in it, with the result that the imprint of the hot iron was tattooed onto the back of the tunic. It was obvious that something was wrong because a singeing smell drifted to the noses of my compatriots, who were very helpful with remedial advice such as, "Rub it hard with half a crown, Scouse. That should clear the burn off." I tried that solution and other methods, but to no avail.

The first parade next day was square bashing dress with best BD boots and gaiters. I dressed accordingly. "How's it look from the back?" I asked several mates.

"Well, you can see it but it's not that bad, I don't think it will be noticed," was the general consensus of opinion. We formed up on the road outside the dormitory. The corporal gave his platoon a quick glance then proceeded to march us on to the Barrack Square. It was very busy this morning. I could see other platoons already lined up on the periphery and still more platoons making their way. I remembered reading on the daily roster the night before, "Company parade and inspection by the CSM". I hadn't fully understood what this meant until now. The platoon corporal gave us last-minute instructions, saying he didn't want any cock-ups. We had only had one period of drill instruction the previous day and were very nervous —

we hardly knew our right from our left. Any cock-ups would reflect on the incompetence of the platoon corporal who could be bawled out for it in front of the whole parade.

The company was standing at ease. The company sergeant major (CSM) stood in the centre of the parade ground, immaculately turned out, and erect in stature. He was a very imposing figure with his Sam Browne belt and peaked cap shading his eyes, his highly polished pacing stick held rigidly under his left arm. He was now about to issue forth a series of commands that would strike terror into the very sinews of all on parade.

"Atteeeenshun!" At this over 250 left legs lifted to their highest point so that the thigh was horizontal and the lower leg vertical; 250 boot-encased left feet then crashed down to rest beside their right boots. It made a most wonderful sound on the surface of the gravelled parade ground.

"Stand still that man!" The eagle-eyed CSM had spotted a slight tremble among the massed ranks.

"Righhhhht markers!" Immediately all the platoon corporals came to attention and marched towards the CSM, where they halted in line abreast.

"Outwards turn!" The corporal on the right of the line stood still, the others turned left.

"Halting at fifteen paces intervals, by the front, quiiick march!" The column of corporals marched ahead, counting quietly to themselves as they went. Each one halted at the correct distance and immediately turned to his right: this was a well-practised manoeuvre.

"Compaaany!" roared the CSM as a command warning. "Get oooon parade!" The word "on" was drawn out purposely because the word that followed it, "parade", was the operative word and it was snapped out sharply. Two hundred and fifty left legs took a pace forward, followed by their right-leg partners. Left right, left right, crunched the boots; left right left swung the arms at shoulder height and in a counter-balancing movement. There was always the danger of marching behind an unfortunate who could not perform this normal synchronisation of movement which could knock you completely out of step and leave a domino effect on those marching behind. As the platoons approached their respective corporals, they would fall in on his left and come to the halt.

"Open orderrrr march!" The front ranks would step forward with their left foot close to their right then slam their left down hard. The rear rank would perform a mirror image of the same, the centre rank would remain still.

"Righhhhht dress!" Right arms would thrust out to touch the shoulder of the man on the right, heads would also turn to the right at the same time the ranks would shuffle to the left. This action spaced out the files to arms' distance and by looking at the chin of the man next but one the ranks would be kept in line. This was the theory, but the final adjustment would be made by the corporals freeing themselves from the right marker position and alternately positioning themselves at the head of the ranks.

When the corporals were satisfied they would march to the front of their platoons.

The CSM would patiently watch the proceedings and occasionally give vent to his opinion: "Corporal Waybehind get a grip of those dozey individuals . . . Corporal Sluggish take that misfit's name." When all the corporals were at the front of their platoons the CSM would give the next command.

"Eyyyyyes front." Arms that were stretched and aching would now fall smartly to sides, and heads would pivot to the front.

"Stand aaaaaaat ease. Stand easy!" The CSM would now make his way purposefully towards No. 1 platoon. On seeing this the corporal would bring his men to attention then inform the CSM that his platoon was ready for his inspection.

The CSM walked along the front rank, then along the middle rank, then the rear, making comments to the khaki-clad individuals, none of which were complimentary. His final words were to the platoon's training corporal: "You will have to get a grip of these idlers, corporal. Their turn-out is just not good enough."

No. 2 Platoon was the next to be inspected, and I stood in the middle rank. The awesome figure of the CSM passed along in front of me and stopped in front of the next trainee.

"Have you shaved this morning, laddie?"

"Yes, Sir."

"Did you use a mirror?"

"Yes, Sir."

"Then use a bloody razor next time, understand?"

"Yes, Sir." Phew! I was glad it wasn't me. The CSM was now making his way along the rear rank.

"What is this I see, Corporal?" He had spotted my burned tunic. "Didn't you inspect your platoon before you brought them on parade?" The corporal was lost for words.

"This is wilful damage to the King's uniform," ranted the CSM. "I want this man charged accordingly immediately this parade is over, and I'll have words with you personally in my office."

After the parade the platoon was marched to a lecture and I was marched to the company office. I was stood on a veranda with other defaulters, awaiting my turn to be charged. This was another experience for me, another first, no doubt with plenty more firsts to come. This was indeed grave enough but I was not unduly worried: although serious in the eyes of the army, these proceedings were at the same time pure comedy. This was open-air theatre and I was part of the cast.

"Hat and belt off!" shouted the orderly sergeant.

"Left turn, left right, left right, left right, halt, left turn!" I now stood in front of an officer who was sitting behind a desk and who proceeded to question me in a calm and elegant voice that was the complete opposite of the non-commissioned officers.

"Are you double two, three two, four nine, four three, Private Kelly?"

"Yiss, Zir."

"You are charged under section one, two, three, four, five, six, seven of King's regulations that on the twentieth day of January nineteen hundred and fifty you wilfully damaged a battledress tunic belonging to His Majesty the King. You will be issued with a replacement and the cost will be deducted from your army pay. Is there anything that you would like to say?"

"Yiss, Zir, I wuz —" My words were abruptly cut short by the orderly sergeant.

"Be quiet, laddie, don't you dare answer the ossifer back, udderwise you'll be on an udder charge."

"March him outside, Sergeant."

"Left turn, left right, left right, left right, halt, left turn, hat and belt on."

I was then marched to the QM stores and reissued with a new tunic. By the time I caught up with the rest of the platoon they were halfway through their trade assessment programme. After my initial quizzing by the programme instructor as to why I was late for his lecture, I was placed at a small table which had displayed on it a variety of disassembled items such as a bicycle pump, an electric bulb holder, a cycle chain, a mortise lock and many other items that were quite familiar to me. We then had a small period of time to reassemble them.

After two weeks of constant parades, lectures, square bashing, PT, medicals and assessments, we were beginning to get the hang of army life. What always sticks in my memory was the evening film in the camp theatre. We had no idea what it was going to be, but we

225

were inclined to think that it would involve the military, and we were correct. It was a War Office propaganda medical film all about venereal diseases. The documentary was most frightening and the pictures horrific. It went through all the known cases of sexually transmitted diseases — we didn't realise there were so many. The most common ones like gonorrhoea and syphilis were lectured upon in great detail. We were shown pictures of men and women with the results of these afflictions over their bodies, and first-, second-, and third-stage syphilis was explained to us. We left the theatre after the show absolutely cowed and frightened out of our wits; it was enough to put you off sex for the rest of your life. The majority of us were young and inexperienced virgins, and as a result of these films would stay that way for some time to come. You have to give it to the military, they certainly know how to drive a message home. And the final warning that came from the film's narrator was that it was a court-martial offence to acquire the self-inflicted disease. This film marked the end of our stay at Parson's Barracks. We were now moved on for more advanced training and so on Friday 2 February 1950 we handed in our bedding, packed our kit and were transported to the 2nd Training Battalion.

Badajoz Barracks, also within the confines of the garrison town of Aldershot, was my next posting. It was a very old cavalry barracks, consisting of two blocks of brick and concrete construction situated either side of a service road. The blocks were three storeys high with barrack rooms running off long open verandas on the first and second floors. The verandas had cast-iron guard rails along their length. The whole frontage of the buildings was open to the elements.

The ground-floor rooms were stores, offices, bath houses, games rooms, cook house and mess rooms. The two blocks were mirror images of each other and they acted like huge echo chambers — the commands of NCOs and the resultant noise of marching feet would be hugely magnified. On the same road, a quarter of a mile distant, stood two more identical blocks called Salamanca, and another quarter of a mile distant Talavera, two more identical twin blocks. These barrack blocks were named after battles fought in the Peninsular War in Spain and commemorated victories won by the Duke of Wellington in 1812.

The British Army is built on tradition, a fact its recruits are constantly reminded of. Tradition is built into uniforms and cap badges, buckles and buttons, indeed everything has nostalgic overtones. I thought life was tough at Parson's Barracks but it was a doddle compared to life at Badajoz. I never felt cold at Parson's — perhaps there was central heating, though I never noticed it. There was certainly no central heating at Badajoz, where each dormitory had a pot-bellied stove in the middle of the room. The stove was immaculate. It shone boot-polish black and the flue pipe was painted white. There was also an empty coal bunker, also painted white, and a galvanised bucket polished to perfection, together with a small shovel. The table in the middle of the room was scrubbed white, as also were the handles of the mop and broom. Even the scrubbing brush was white as the result of continual scraping with old razor blades. The wooden floors were polished with a bumper, a heavy metallic object with a long handle. We each had an iron bed, at the foot of which was a wooden box with a lid about 2ft by 1ft by 1ft. This was our personal locker in which we had to store all our kit except our greatcoat, which was neatly folded in such a way that it resembled a round tube and hung at the back of our bed together with our best BD. On the iron rack above the beds we placed our webbing equipment, helmet, mess tins and tea mug. When we collected our bedding we were also issued with an earthenware mug and told its cost would be deducted from our pay. Most of the mugs were chipped and cracked but nobody really minded about this. On our made-up blanket roll stood our spare pair of boots, with the tops turned inwards and the soles uppermost. The soles were highly polished and displayed thirteen regulation metal studs in each boot — the army was not superstitious. The usual information was pinned on the notice board: fire precautions, reveille, lights out, work rota and training roster. We were soon to be introduced to our platoon corporal, company sergeant and sergeant major.

"Stand by your beds!" bellowed the CSM on entering the room. We hurriedly came to attention at the foot of our beds. "I am your company sergeant major. My name is Smashem and this is your training Corporal Knockemintoshape and this is Sergeant Backmeup." The CSM stopped in front of my trembling frame: "What's your name, laddie?"

"4943 Private Kelly, Sir."

"Very good! It's nice to see that you can remember your name, and that goes for the rest of you. At any time you may be asked your name, rank and number even if it is only by the enemy, so it is most important that you remember it." He then systematically went along the length of the room looking at our equipment on the iron racking. He was carrying his swagger cane in his right hand. When he spotted a tea mug that did not conform to his image of how a mug should be he would immediately whack it with his cane, at the same time uttering mouthfuls of abuse and emphasising each word.

"I — will — not — have — cracked — chipped — or — handless — mugs — in — my — company." The targeted mugs would either be reduced to small pieces on the spot or fly through the air and smash to smithereens on making impact with the floor. "Corporal, you are responsible in seeing that the men's tea mugs are sound and free from flaws. I don't want to have to repeat this operation." But he did because on later visits to the barrack room he found mugs that were facing the wrong way.

"The — handles — of — mugs — will — all — face — the — same — way — that — is — towards — the — exit — door. Corporal, march these men to the CQMS and make sure they buy new mugs."

We had been formally introduced to our new training team, who we were not likely to forget.

It was a bitterly cold night and we were freezing. We needed the pot-bellied stove to be lit, but the problem was that whoever lit it would be responsible for making sure that it was returned to its pristine glory the following morning, and that included repainting the flue stack. We all agreed that the positives were outweighed by the negatives and decided to go to bed early once our allotted duties had been completed.

The 2nd Training Battalion was made up of four companies of trainees, two companies in Badajoz and two companies in Salamanca, one company to a barrack block. Each company had eight platoons of thirty men. There was also an HQ company of permanent training staff. I only did two guard-cum-fire picket duties while I was at Badajoz because of the large numbers of trainees to choose from, which of course was done strictly in alphabetical order. Part of my duties while on prowler patrol was to check that a small central heating boiler for the officers' mess was always well stoked with coal. I made regular visits to this little boiler room in order to comply and as it was February and the nights were cold I would prolong my visits to the fullest extent. The length of training was to be eight weeks and we became better at it as we gained confidence and pride, especially when we witnessed new intakes of trainees coming in from Parson's and noticed how raw they looked. Every intake had a number, which was handy when talking to others because by asking their intake number, you knew which was senior. My intake number was 5002, which meant that I was part of the second intake in 1950. There was movement every two weeks with one company of men arriving and another company of men departing to regular postings as they finished their training and passed out.

We were introduced to the Lee Enfield .303 bolt action rifle and spent many hours learning how to handle it on the parade ground. Marching with a rifle was something different. We learned how to throw it about our bodies with confidence on the commands of our corporal: sloping arms, presenting arms, ordering arms, saluting on the march and so on. When we had mastered these skills we were taught how to strip it down, clean it, load and unload it, aim it and gently squeeze the trigger. The final art was to fire, and to learn this skill we went to the army's firing range in Hampshire on many occasions. The whole company would be involved, taking it in turn to fire in a prone position at the firing point or in the butts raising and lowering the mechanical targets and pasting up the bullet holes. When we were proficient with the rifle we were introduced to the Bren machine gun, and later still the automatic Sten gun. Then we had bayonet practice, charging across open ground screaming and bayoneting a swinging sandbag. It was all good fun, but some of us were better at screaming than others; it depended on what sort of upbringing you had endured. If you didn't scream viciously enough you soon got to know about it. "Private Whisper, open your mouth wide and scream damn you, scream! I want to see that sandbag take fright and run for its life."

Cross-country runs with full pack were a regular feature of our training. The NCOs were always looking for skivvies to help in the cookhouses and they would devise ways of entrapping them, the usual one being last one/two/three to fall in on muster parade. Sometimes we would have to race the length of the barrack square and return with the threat of what would happen to the stragglers — you had to be fit to survive.

Whenever you visited the NAAFI for your tea break there would always be somebody from a very good home practising on the piano. He would be taking the opportunity to perform his skills in front of a large captive audience. The recruits came from all walks of life, from good homes and not so good homes, from wealthy families and not so wealthy. Some were extremely bright and others were not so bright, and among these individuals were some of officer material. Close at hand was an officer cadre school, which had potential officers who had been plucked from the ragbag of raw recruits.

The officers' mess, which had its own kitchen, would also require skivvies to wash greasy pans, but they preferred a more cultured lackey. On parade one day the sergeant major says to the assembled company: "The officers' mess are looking for musicians. All those who have a musical talent such as playing the piano, violin, trombone, or any other instrument, please take one pace forward." Immediately, a dozen or so recruits from various platoons happily obeyed the sergeant major's command. "Corporals! Take those men's names and submit them to the company office." The officers' mess catering sergeant now had a reservoir of high-class skivvies at his beck and call, and the would-be musicians were in for a terrible shock.

The small locker at the foot of our beds had to be packed in such a way that we could retrieve any item at a moment's notice, even in complete darkness, and yet leave the room in perfect order. This occurred every time we changed from one mode of dress to another, which was mostly after each programme. After being marched to the billet we would be instructed to change into the appropriate kit for our next activity, with the usual warning that the last on parade would be on fatigues that evening. On dismissal there would be a stampede of bodies racing up the iron steps, dashing into the billet, changing clothing then dashing down again to form up on the road. Some unfortunates never seemed to get the hang of it and were always the last ones to appear. Even the quickest could never expect to miss fatigue duties, as sometimes the corporal or sergeant would come along at the last minute and nab the first ones that came into view. I remember washing greasy pans in lukewarm water in the officers' mess cookhouse. On another occasion, I was sitting in a circle with eight others, peeling a mountain of spuds that were dumped on the floor in front of us. As we peeled them with our jackknives we would throw them into huge dixies. One bright spark said we'd get through this lot quicker if we peeled them thicker, so this we did. When we were reaching the bottom of the pile the cook sergeant appeared and with an experienced eye noticed that the spuds in the dixies had many angles to them and also the peelings were rather thick. He then split us into two groups, making the first group peel the peelings and the second a new mountain of potatoes that were dumped before us.

Once every eight weeks there would be a huge full dress parade, at which the whole battalion was present. It was conducted by the regimental sergeant major (RSM). Each of the four companies present would be in varying degrees of training, some having just come from Parson's Barracks, others about to be posted elsewhere to permanent positions. A military band would form up on one side of the square, and the RSM would inspect the parade, going from platoon to platoon, from company to company, and issuing forth admonishments as he saw fit. Finally, he would give the command for the battalion to move off: "By the riiight . . . quiiiick march." Over 1,000 men stepped off on their left feet, bodies erect and with heads looking forward yet their eyes glancing to the right in order to keep their dressing. At the same instant the band struck up with an uplifting military march, and we swaggered to the rhythm of the big bass drum. It's a most wonderful feeling to proudly march with a battalion of men to the stirring sound of military music, and something I will never forget.

The day was approaching for my Company, B Coy, to experience passing out parade. We bulled our kit like never before. We had to carry field service marching order (FSMO) which was best BD and boots, large pack, small pack, ammunition pouches, cross braces, waterbottle, rifle and bayonet. Our packs were to be loaded with our clothing and we carried our greatcoats

234

across the top of our large pack. We lined up on the road outside the barrack block; the most nervous of our platoon was the corporal. He was like a mother hen running about adjusting our webbing. Eventually we marched on to the Barrack Square, where the RSM was now in full control. A host of commissioned officers of various ranks, the most notable being the commanding officer, were present. The officers wore their number one uniform and carried ceremonial swords. Not every platoon was inspected in the same fashion. Some had to open their small packs and lay the contents neatly onto the parade ground, others had to empty their large packs. This procedure took quite some time to implement, and by the time it was our turn to be inspected, the colonel gave us a very quick look over then spoke to the RSM.

The result of this conversation turned the RSM into a rage. He turned to our platoon corporal and said, "I have never seen such a ghastly turn-out as this. These men are an absolute shower, march them off, Corporal, and bring them back in proper order and minus their webbing equipment in one hour." We were absolutely gutted: this was supposed to be our passing out parade and we had failed it. We were marched to the NAAFI by the corporal and dismissed for a twenty-minute break. Instead of being agitated, the corporal seemed quite calm about it all.

"Don't worry," he said. "The Colonel was probably getting tired and wanted an excuse for a coffee break. After you have had a cuppa, we'll march back to the block, take off the webbing and tidy ourselves up. Then we'll report to the square again."

We formed up very apprehensively on the Barrack Square, and the RSM approached us in league with a host of officers and the colonel. After what appeared to be a very brief inspection without any rebuffs, the RSM announced that the colonel was very pleased with our turn-out. He also said he would be on the lookout for potential squad instructors, and finished off by asking was anybody prepared to volunteer for active service in the Far East? If they were then they were to take one step forward. I, together with five others, took one step forward. The rest of the platoon thought we were stark raving mad, but it ultimately proved to be the correct decision. I was very happy now that I had passed out because I was now a soldier of the king. There were volunteers from other platoons and we were all placed together to form a new squad. We had to serve for another four weeks in Badajoz to do extra training: this was called a Far East Land Forces course (FARELF). None of us minded because we knew what the end result would be. Companions who I had trained with for over two months and got to understand were now dispersed and posted to all sorts of other units. I learned that this was part and parcel of army life, a continual bonding and breaking of friendships brought about by the endless movement of personnel.

This was to be a relaxing and happy four weeks. The soldiers of the FARELF course had grown in stature and we were now the senior platoon in the battalion. We were looked up to by the other trainees and held in awe by new intakes from Parson's Barracks. We did a lot of field craft, weapon training, firearms shooting and survival training, which included outdoor cooking. For this the cook sergeant took control and we were grouped into fours and prepared meals in our mess tins over open fires. The name of the dish was "throw-it-in-the-pan" — there was no culinary skills involved, no messing about. You just threw it in the pot and stewed it. This was good fun and the lads enjoyed it. Finally, we were told that we were going to Malaya, which was a trouble spot on the world map. Malaya and Singapore were then part of the British Empire. There was a large British garrison there already who were constantly under threat by communist insurgents fighting for their independence.

During my period of military training at Badajoz there was a docks dispute throughout Britain and we were warned that we could be used to assist the unloading of ships in the port of London. I am very glad that the dispute was resolved and we were stood down; I had visions of Dad on the picket lines in Liverpool while his son was being used to break the conflict in London. I was in a mental dilemma: I would have been a traitor to my own working-class father.

After we had all completed our four-week FARELF course we received a series of inoculations for typhoid fever, yellow fever and other diseases that do not spring to mind. Apart from a stiff arm the inoculations did not affect me, but some of the lads were really ill and had to stay in the sick bay for a few days while their bodies readjusted. Finally, we packed our kit and moved out of Badajoz for the last time.

Feltham Transit Camp, in Middlesex, was our temporary posting. We now received two weeks' embarkation leave, so the young and proud soldier headed straight home by train to see his Mam and Dad and family. The first thing Dad said to me as I entered the front door was: "When are you going back, son?" This was not meant in malice; he really meant, "How long have you got before you return to your unit?" In fact it was a phrase I would often hear from family and friends.

I know that Mam was glad to see me although as usual she did not say much: she was her usual non-demonstrative self. Dad was now forty-nine, Mam forty-two, Monica nineteen, I was eighteen, Gerald fifteen, Peter twelve, Irene five and Chris three. It was nice to be home and mix with the family again, but I was keen and eager to be off and see the world. Dad tried to coax me to Gleeson's, his local, for a couple of pints but at this period of my life alcohol had never touched my lips and neither had cigarettes. I remember saying to Dad, "If they sold pints of milk in pubs then I would come with you."

When the time came to go I said my goodbyes to brothers and sisters, and Mam, as undemonstrative as ever said "Be careful, son," I know how she felt because I was her eldest son. Dad took me by the hand and told me to look after myself. I had always reminded Dad of his eldest brother John who was killed on the Somme in the First World War. I knew Dad was sad, although he didn't show it. He had seen his brother sail to France in 1916 and never return. But a young virile man knows nothing of deep emotion, he just has a zest for adventure and a passion for excitement, and I am sure that Uncle John must have felt the same in those far-off days, even if he was going to face the enemy.

On returning to Feltham we were impregnated with more hypodermic needles and issued with more kit and another kitbag to put it in: this was known as our sea bag. Lightweight jungle greens or olive greens as they were sometimes referred to, long and short trousers, hose tops with flashes and puttees, lightweight vests and underpants, a floppy hat and a poncho. We stayed in Feltham for about two weeks. They kept us busy doing fatigues — I was mostly gardening. One morning we packed all our kit and were transported to the rail station and boarded a military train. We were all very excited when the train reached its destination, Southampton. We stood on the dockside looking in amazement at the huge white hull of a ship with a broad blue band painted along its side and on the stern the name HMT *Empire Fowey*. We were given free cups of tea and biscuits from a mobile stall by smiling ladies wearing navy blue bonnets encircled with red ribbons. They were from the Salvation Army — what a wonderful and charitable organisation that is.

There were thousands of troops waiting to board this huge ship and they came from a variety of regiments. There were also WAAFS and WRACS and married families. As we stood around absorbing the colourful panoramic scene — even though it was mostly khaki —

we pondered on the letters before the ship's name. The answer came along the grapevine: HMT meant His Majesty's Trooper. In my simplicity I thought "blimey, does the king own everything?" Eventually the time came for our lot to climb the gangplank and board this floating hotel. We then went below decks to our appointed sleeping quarters. We slept in standees, two-tier metal bunks. Our main kitbag was stored in the ship's hold, and all the kit we needed for our voyage was kept with us in the sea bag, plus a bed roll and pillow that was issued to us on board. We were also issued with a coloured plastic disc, which was our meal ticket. The ship's tannoy system was our communicator and there were loudspeakers in all parts of the ship. All important information was announced this way. At mealtimes the tannoy would announce: "Blue discs to the cafeteria now." On entering the cafeteria your blue disc would be exchanged for a red one. You would pick up an indented tray and be served your meal as you progressed along the servery. The food was first class and could not be faulted. As the queue diminished the tannoy would announce: "Green discs to the cafeteria now." Green discs would be exchanged for yellow discs. The final colour was white for black. It was a well-organised system, without any cock-ups and there was never a shortage of cooked food. The troops were well looked after and it was a very happy ship to sail on.

That evening the troop ship pulled away, assisted by the strength of ocean-going tug boats. Thousands of troops lined her rails watching the distance between ship and shore expand as the stirring sounds from the

Royal Marines Band playing on the quayside drifted across Southampton Water in a parting gesture of farewell. As we sailed into the Solent we experienced the customary lifeboat drill and were made aware of our boat stations. Certain individuals were picked for fatigues but for the first week I was a free man with nothing to do but admire the ever-changing scene and soak up the sun, for as the troopship sailed in a southerly direction the skies became less cloudy and the temperature began to rise appreciably. We were now ordered to change into tropical kit, with shorts, and to wear our long trousers only when the sun went down. This was acceptable: in the army you cannot wear what you would like, you wear what you are told to wear. It was now getting increasingly warm in the evening and on the troop decks it was uncomfortable when trying to sleep. We were told that those who wanted to sleep on deck could do so. I tried this and found it very satisfactory — until the seas began to rise and sprayed the deck with cold salt water.

Every morning after ablutions were completed our standees would be hooked up vertically, our bed roll and sea bag stored away and the lower troop decks vacated except for fatigue parties. When the boat was shipshape and Bristol fashion the captain would do his rounds, inspecting all parts of the ship. Only when he was completely satisfied with the cleanliness of his command could we return to our troop decks.

A favourite game we played on the open deck was push penny football. Matchsticks were stuck into the tarred joints between deck planks to act as goal posts, then with a penny and a comb we would try to score by knocking a tanner into the opponent's net. The game involved only two players at a time but it was as exciting for the onlookers as it was for the players because side bets were made as to the outcome of the timed match. It was like being at a proper football game, with the deafening roar of the crowd. Such games were constantly played all over the decks.

We were kept active with PT sessions and interregimental tug of war contests. This could be a bit tricky, since with the pitch and roll of the ship your caller had to time things correctly to gain the advantage. Our team got as far as the semi-finals, then disaster struck; the opposing team had the advantage as the ship dipped and they were pulling downhill. We ended up on the gunwales and one of our team made contact with the wheel of a fire valve, which opened: the deck was flooded and we got swept off our feet. On other occasions, usually in the evenings, a boxing ring was rigged up on the hatch covers and interregimental boxing took place. I entered as a middleweight and got as far as the final but then I met more than my match. Boxing on a level playing field is hard enough, but when the ring is rotating, to cope with the roll and pitch of the ship, that one mistimed punch can be your last chance. I was fighting a rugged and well-built boxer who I surmise was in his mid-twenties. He was exceptionally good and his facial features conveyed his pugilistic experience. I never saw the punch coming that put me to the canvas.

Also available in ISIS Large Print:

Bockety

Desmond Ellis

"The only people who aren't bockety are the ones who don't worry about anything. And the only people who don't worry about anything are simple-minded, and you can't get more bockety than that, can you?"

Bockety **adjective** Irish rickety, unstable, lopsided, crooked

Born in 1944, Desmond Ellis grew up on the banks of the Grand Canal in Dublin. This slightly awkward first-born child romps through his childhood like a bockety bicycle that won't quite go where it is steered. His playground is the Grand Canal, where he goes crashing through the reeds with fishing nets. At home he washes off the inevitable grime in a tin tub by the fire, and the toilet is a draughty shed in the yard.

Bockety is a tale of a time of few cars and many bicycles. Gratification was to be had in Cleeve's toffee and gobstoppers. And then there was the terrible confusion of girls . . .

ISBN 978-0-7531-9424-9 (hb)
ISBN 978-0-7531-9425-6 (pb)

Huddersfield at War

Hazel Wheeler

"Many neighbours arranged to dash into each other's shelters on alternate alerts. It gave them a bit more chance to gossip."

Hazel Wheeler looks at life in Huddersfield during the Second World War. From rationing and the extra work that this involved for her shopkeeper father, to the working lives of men and women, this is an absorbing look at how the people of Huddersfield coped with the war. With a real sense of a community banding together, Hazel collects wartime stories of playing games while waiting for the all clear, of knitting for the troops and of the joy of VE day.

ISBN 978-0-7531-9416-4 (hb)
ISBN 978-0-7531-9417-1 (pb)